I0704882

Fascinating Facts About the Animal Kingdom

Discover 600+ Surprising Animal Facts with Verified References for Curious Children and Adults

by

Vladimir Cejzl

Copyright

————————— ◆ —————————

Copyright © 2024 Vladimir Cejzl. All rights reserved.

No part of this publication may be reproduced, distributed, or transmitted in any form or by any means, including photocopying, recording, or any electronic or mechanical methods, without the prior written permission of the copyright holder, except for brief quotations in book reviews with proper attribution.

The facts in this book are presented as reported in scientific journals, academic publications, and verified sources at the time of publication. The author and publisher make no warranties regarding the accuracy, completeness, or currentness of the information contained herein. Science is continually evolving, and readers are encouraged to verify any critical information or claims independently.

Images used throughout this book are selected for educational and illustrative purposes. Some images are original works digitally created for this publication and are the copyright of Vladimir Cejzl. Others are sourced under applicable licenses. Due to copyright, licensing, or availability considerations, images may not precisely represent the specific subjects, locations, or events described in the accompanying facts.

————————— ◆ —————————

THIS BOOK IS PART OF

THE FUN & INTRIGUING FACTS BOOKS SERIES

Content

Welcome To Facts You Can Actually Trust

———— ◆ ————

In a world flooded with viral myths and unverified "facts," this Series stands apart by delivering True Verified Facts – 100% research-backed knowledge from the world's most prestigious sources.

What makes the Fun & Intriguing Facts Books Series different is that every single fact in these books has been meticulously verified through academic publications, peer-reviewed scientific journals, and leading research institutions, including MIT, Stanford, NASA, and other authoritative sources.

Explore the Fun & Intriguing Facts Books Series Collection:

Earth & Space Phenomena | AI & Technology | Money & Economics
Flora & Botanical Wonders | Wildlife & Nature | Weather Science
Lunar Mysteries | Sports Achievements | Time & Traditions
...and many more fascinating topics!

———— ◆ ————

**COLLECT THE FUN & INTRIGUING FACTS BOOKS SERIES.
EXPAND YOUR MIND. TRUST WHAT YOU LEARN**

Free Books

———————— ◆ ————————

EXCLUSIVELY FOR READERS OF THIS SERIES — NEVER SOLD, NEVER LISTED ANYWHERE.

<u>FREE E-BOOKS</u>

Fascinating Facts About Love & Desire

From ancient rituals to modern psychology — history's most intimate subject, verified and uncensored. The kind of facts you don't forget at dinner.

Fascinating Facts About Unsolved Murders

Cold cases, serial killers, and crimes that baffled the FBI. Research-backed true crime facts from the darkest files in criminal history.

<u>TO CLAIM YOUR FREE E-BOOKS:</u>
EMAIL: **fascinatingfacts@icloud.com**
SUBJECT: **Free Books**
INCLUDE: **Your first name**
No spam. No obligations. Unsubscribe anytime.

———————— ◆ ————————

TRUE VERIFIED FACTS • FUN & INTRIGUING FACTS BOOKS SERIES

Introduction

Did you know that 500,000 starlings can move as a single shape-shifting body in the sky — with no leader, no signal, and no plan — each bird following just three rules?

You are about to discover one of the most extraordinary collections of verified animal science assembled. These are True Verified Facts — every entry backed by peer-reviewed research from institutions including Nature, PNAS, the Smithsonian, and Cornell University.

Inside, you will learn why a bombardier beetle fires a 212°F chemical pulse from a rotating nozzle, how army ants vote, why vampire bats keep score across hundreds of favors, and what a crow at Oxford University proved about bird intelligence that stunned the scientific world.

From the oldest animal fossil on Earth to the smallest vertebrate hiding in a rainforest leaf until 2009, every page reveals another chapter of life that feels too strange to be real.

Let's explore the science behind the creatures that share this planet with us.

The Story of Animal Life

☑ How Old Is Life on Earth? The oldest confirmed evidence of life is stromatolite fossils — layered microbial mats — dating to 3.5 billion BCE in Western Australia. Animals arrived much later: the first did not appear until roughly 600 million BCE, meaning microbes ruled Earth for nearly three billion years before animals evolved. (Source: Nature, 1987)

☑ What Exactly Makes Something an Animal? Animals are multicellular organisms that eat other living organisms rather than photosynthesize. They have specialized cells, move at some life stage, and typically reproduce sexually. Even sponges, which have no nerves or organs, qualify, making the biological definition far broader than most people imagine. (Source: Encyclopedia of Life Sciences, 2010)

☑ What Made Complex Animal Life Possible? Around 2.4 billion BCE, cyanobacteria began releasing oxygen as a metabolic byproduct, transforming Earth's atmosphere. For anaerobic life, it was catastrophic. For future animals, it was essential. The high-energy metabolism required to run, hunt, and think is physically impossible without a richly oxygenated atmosphere. (Source: Nature Geoscience, 2009)

☑ **Did Life Almost End Before Animals Even Began?** Between roughly 720 and 635 million BCE, glaciers extended to the equator in what scientists call Snowball Earth. Multicellular life survived in liquid water beneath the ice. The subsequent thaw dramatically increased atmospheric oxygen — creating the conditions that enabled the Cambrian Explosion of animal life. (Source: Nature, 2000)

☑ **Where Did the Energy Engines of Animal Cells Come From?** Mitochondria — the powerhouses of every animal cell — were once free-living bacteria. Around 1.5 billion BCE, an ancient cell engulfed one without digesting it, forming a permanent partnership. The bacterium became the mitochondrion. This endosymbiotic event supplied the energy output that complex animal life depends upon. (Source: PNAS, 1967)

☑ **How Did Single Cells Become Complex Animals?** Multicellularity evolved independently in animals, plants, and fungi. The critical leap for animals was cells specializing rather than competing — dividing labor into muscle, nerve, and reproductive tissue. Genetic evidence shows that the cell-adhesion mechanisms making multicellularity possible predate the first animals by hundreds of millions of years. (Source: Cell, 2019)

☑ **What Lived Before the Cambrian Explosion?** The Ediacaran period (635–541 million BCE) produced Earth's earliest complex multicellular animals: soft-bodied creatures like Dickinsonia and Charnia with no heads, limbs, or mouths as we know them. They left no descendants. These organisms represent a biological experiment that dissolved before modern animal life began. (Source: Nature, 2018)

☑ **What Is the Oldest Known Animal Fossil?** Dickinsonia, a flat oval creature, was confirmed as an animal in 2018 when scientists extracted cholesterol — a molecule exclusive to animal cells — from 558-million-year-old Russian fossils. Before that discovery, whether it was animal, plant, or fungus had been debated for over 75 years. (Source: Science, 2018)

☑ **Why Do Most Animals Have Two Matching Sides?** Bilateral symmetry — one body with mirrored halves — evolved around 600 million BCE and dominates the animal kingdom. It allows directed movement, paired sense organs, and a centralized brain at the front end. Animals built symmetrically can sense and flee threats more effectively than any other body plan. (Source: Trends in Ecology and Evolution, 2008)

☑ **When Did Animal Diversity Suddenly Explode?** Around 541 million BCE, nearly every major animal body plan appeared within roughly 25 million years — a blink in geological time. Before this Cambrian Explosion, animal life was sparse and simple. After it, the seas filled with predators, prey, and body architectures that persist to this day. (Source: Smithsonian Institution, 2013)

☑ **How Does the Battle Between Predator and Prey Drive Evolution?** Predator-prey relationships create self-escalating arms races: prey develop faster legs or thicker shells; predators evolve stronger jaws or better eyesight in response. Each adaptation by one side forces a counter-adaptation by the other. This biological tension drives biodiversity — complexity breeds further complexity. (Source: Evolution, 2014)

☑ **What Actually Triggered the Cambrian Explosion?** No single cause is confirmed, but leading hypotheses include rising oxygen, expanding shallow seas after glacial retreat, the first evolution of predation, and ocean chemistry changes enabling calcium shells. Most researchers believe it was a cascade: each new innovation unlocked further possibilities, compounding into an irreversible biological revolution. (Source: Annual Review of Ecology, Evolution, and Systematics, 2011)

☑ **Why Did Cambrian Animals Suddenly Grow Shells?** At the Cambrian Explosion's onset, animals began producing calcium carbonate skeletons for the first time. Rising ocean calcium and the emergence of predation made armor instantly advantageous. Hard parts also fossilize far more readily than soft tissue — explaining why the fossil record sharpens dramatically at this boundary. (Source: Paleontology, 2014)

☑ **What Does Canada's Burgess Shale Reveal?** This Rocky Mountain fossil site preserves Cambrian life from 508 million BCE in extraordinary detail — including soft tissues that rarely survive fossilization. Creatures like Anomalocaris and Hallucigenia, with no modern relatives, appear here intact: a window into the full, strange breadth of early animal life. (Source: Geological Survey of Canada, 1986)

☑ **Which Animals First Evolved Eyes?** Trilobites, ancient marine arthropods, developed compound eyes around 521 million BCE — among the first visual systems in animal history. Their calcite lenses were so optically precise that their design principles inform modern camera engineering. Sight gave predators and prey a decisive new advantage, transforming how natural selection operated. (Source: Nature, 2019)

☑ **Why Did So Many Cambrian Animals Vanish?** Creatures like Hallucigenia — with spines defying categorization — and Opabinia — with five eyes and a frontal grasping limb — represent evolutionary experiments with no modern descendants. Their extinction illustrates evolution's reality: most body plans ever attempted have been discarded. The animals alive today are survivors of a brutal filter. (Source: Smithsonian Institution, 2012)

☑ **What Genes Build Every Animal Body?** Hox genes are master switches determining head-to-tail organization in virtually all animals. Fruit flies and humans share the same core toolkit. Alter one Hox gene in a fly and legs grow where antennae should be — evidence that evolution builds radically different bodies from a shared ancient blueprint. (Source: Science, 1995)

☑ **Why Do Sharks and Dolphins Look Almost Identical?** These animals share virtually no ancestry, yet evolved the same torpedo body, dorsal fin, and powerful tail independently. This is convergent evolution: natural selection arriving at the same solution separately. Ocean physics is so demanding that only one body shape works for large, fast predators. (Source: Journal of Evolutionary Biology, 2015)

☑ **How Old Are the Genes That Build Animal Bodies?** The Hox gene system is estimated to be over 600 million years old, predating the Cambrian Explosion. The blueprint for complex bodies existed before most animals did — confirming that evolution's toolkit was assembled long before the animals that use it came to exist. (Source: PNAS, 2003)

☑ **How Many Times Did Eyes Evolve Independently?** Eyes evolved at least 40 separate times in the animal kingdom — in vertebrates, mollusks, insects, and jellyfish — through different genetic and structural pathways each time. Yet the core light-detecting protein, opsin, appears across nearly every eye type, suggesting evolution repeatedly reused the same ancient photosensitive chemistry. (Source: Proceedings of the Royal Society B, 2013)

☑ **What First Crawled Out of the Sea?** Tiktaalik roseae, discovered on Canada's Ellesmere Island in 2004, lived approximately 375 million BCE. This "fishapod" had fins strong enough to support body weight — functioning like primitive arms — and a mobile neck unique among fish. It marks the evolutionary moment when vertebrates first moved from water to land. (Source: Nature, 2006)

☑ **How Did Animals Move From the Ocean Into the Rivers?** Freshwater is less dense than blood, unlike seawater, forcing cells to expel excess water through osmosis constantly. Solving this challenge required new physiological machinery. Groups that managed it — fish, crustaceans, mollusks — colonized freshwater independently and repeatedly, producing many of the riverine species that exist today. (Source: Annual Review of Ecology, 2009)

☑ **How Did Moving Continents Shape Evolution?** Continental drift isolated populations, creating separate gene pools that diverged into new species. When South America separated from Africa roughly 100 million BCE, shared ancestors evolved independently on each continent. Australia's iconic fauna — marsupials and monotremes — is a direct product of 80 million years of isolation. (Source: Annual Review of Earth and Planetary Sciences, 2017)

☑ **Did Flight Evolve Just Once in the Animal Kingdom?** Powered flight evolved at least four times independently: insects (~350 million BCE), pterosaurs (~228 million BCE), birds (~150 million BCE from feathered dinosaurs), and bats (~50 million BCE). Each lineage solved the physics of lift through entirely different anatomical structures — yet all four succeeded. (Source: Annual Review of Ecology, Evolution, and Systematics, 2015)

☑ **How Did Dinosaurs Become Birds?** Feathers evolved in theropod dinosaurs millions of years before flight — initially for insulation and display. Archaeopteryx, from roughly 150 million BCE, preserves the transitional form: birdlike feathers, clawed wings, and a reptilian tail. By every rigorous modern classification, today's birds are a surviving lineage of dinosaurs. (Source: Nature, 2011)

☑ **Did Warm Blood Evolve Once or Multiple Times?** Endothermy — the ability to generate internal heat — evolved independently in mammals and birds, and possibly in some extinct marine reptiles. It arose at least twice. The payoff: warm-blooded animals can survive cold environments and maintain activity levels impossible for cold-blooded equivalents. (Source: Science, 2016)

☑ **When Did Animals and Plants Part Ways?** Animals and plants share a single-celled common ancestor. Molecular clock studies place the divergence at approximately 1 billion BCE, when one lineage evolved to harvest sunlight and another to consume other organisms. For most of Earth's history, every future animal and plant was the same cell. (Source: Nature, 2004)

☑ **How Much Does Being Warm-Blooded Cost?** Maintaining constant body temperature requires roughly 10 times more food than a cold-blooded animal of equal size. A mouse and a lizard of the same mass have entirely different caloric needs. This is why warm-blooded animals must eat frequently, and why metabolic rate, not size, governs hunger. (Source: Physiological and Biochemical Zoology, 2004)

☑ **When Did the First Nervous System Appear?** Cnidarians — jellyfish and sea anemones — have the simplest known nervous systems: diffuse nerve nets with no central brain, dating to at least 560 million BCE. Bilaterally symmetrical animals later centralized these into their brains. The nervous system's evolution is inseparable from the emergence of complex behavior. (Source: Nature Reviews Neuroscience, 2008)

☑ **What Does a Sea Sponge's DNA Tell Us?** The genome of Amphimedon queenslandica, a simple sea sponge, contains genes linked to nerve-cell signaling — despite sponges having no nervous system. This suggests the genetic toolkit for complex animal bodies predates the animals themselves, assembled and waiting long before evolution found ways to deploy it. (Source: Nature, 2010)

☑ **Why Does Sexual Reproduction Make Evolution Faster?** Sexual reproduction shuffles genetic material every generation, producing offspring with novel combinations. This constant remixing allows populations to adapt to parasites, diseases, and environmental changes far faster than clonal reproduction. The resulting genetic variation is the raw material natural selection acts upon — the engine of evolutionary speed. (Source: Science, 2011)

☑ Why Are Insects the Most Successful Animals? With roughly one million named species and an estimated 5.5 million total, insects represent over half of all animal life. Powered flight, rapid reproduction, and desiccation-resistant exoskeletons drove their dominance. They colonized land before any vertebrate — and have never relinquished their lead. (Source: PLOS ONE, 2022)

☑ Can Animals Thrive Without Sunlight? Hydrothermal vents on the deep ocean floor, discovered in 1977, sustain entire animal ecosystems powered by chemosynthesis rather than sunlight. Tube worms up to 7 feet (2.1 m) long and eyeless shrimp flourish near water at 750 degrees F (400 degrees C). Life — and evolution — needs no sun. (Source: Science, 1979)

☑ Which Mass Extinction Was the Worst Ever? The Permian extinction, 252 million BCE, eliminated approximately 96% of all marine species and 70% of terrestrial vertebrates — far dwarfing the asteroid impact that killed the dinosaurs. Scientists link it to massive volcanic eruptions in present-day Siberia that triggered runaway global ocean acidification. (Source: Science, 2012)

☑ Which Animals Diversified at Record Speed? Cichlid fish in Africa's Great Lakes produced over 500 species from a single ancestor in under 15,000 years — among the fastest evolutionary radiations ever documented. After the K-Pg extinction, placental mammals staged a comparable burst, diversifying from a handful of survivors into the world's modern mammal fauna. (Source: Science, 2006)

☑ How Many Animal Species Exist on Earth? Scientists estimate approximately 8.7 million animal species on Earth, yet only about 1.5 million have been formally named. The majority remain undiscovered — primarily in the deep ocean and tropical forests. At the current pace of taxonomy, cataloging all life on Earth would require over 1,000 years. (Source: PLoS Biology, 2011)

☑ How Did an Asteroid Create the Age of Mammals? The K-Pg extinction, 66 million BCE, eliminated approximately 76% of all species, including non-avian dinosaurs. The vacant ecological niches allowed small, nocturnal mammals to diversify at an extraordinary speed. Within 10 million years, mammals had occupied every major habitat on Earth, from the deep ocean to the high canopy. (Source: Science, 2013)

☑ Do Mass Extinctions Help Evolution in the Long Run? Mass extinctions clear dominant species and free ecological space, enabling surviving lineages to diversify rapidly. Following each of the five recognized mass extinctions, biodiversity eventually surpassed pre-extinction levels, though recovery typically required five to ten million years. Catastrophe, in evolutionary terms, reliably produces reinvention. (Source: PNAS, 2015)

☑ How Did the Platypus Challenge Animal Classification? When Ornithorhynchus anatinus was described in 1799, it violated every existing taxonomic rule: a mammal that lays eggs, has a bill detecting electrical fields, and — in males — venomous ankle spurs. It belongs to monotremes, a 166-million-year old lineage at the base of the mammalian family tree. (Source: Journal of Natural History, 2002)

☑ What Percentage of All Animals Are Now Extinct? Scientists estimate that approximately 99% of all animal species that have ever lived are now extinct. With roughly 8.7 million alive today, over four billion species have come and gone. Extinction is not the exception in animal history — it is the overwhelming rule. (Source: Wilson, E.O.; IUCN, 2002)

Senses Beyond Imagination

☑ How Do Bats Hunt in Total Darkness? Bats emit ultrasonic pulses between 20,000 and 200,000 Hz and interpret returning echoes with millisecond precision. The big brown bat fires up to 200 clicks per second during a final attack run. Some species can detect a wire 0.28 mm in diameter in complete darkness. (Source: Journal of Experimental Biology, 2000)

☑ What Is the Fastest-Foraging Mammal on Earth? The star-nosed mole's 22 pink tentacles contain over 25,000 Eimer's organs — minute sensory receptors. It can detect, identify, and consume a small invertebrate in under 120 milliseconds, faster than the human eye can track. Its nose processes touch at the same speed our eyes process light. (Source: Nature Neuroscience, 2006)

☑ How Does Dolphin Sonar Compare to Bat Echolocation? Both use biosonar, but dolphin clicks reach 220 decibels — far louder than any bat. Dolphins calculate an object's shape, distance, speed, and texture from a single returning echo. They achieve this precision in water, a medium acoustically far more complex than air. (Source: PNAS, 2004)

☑ Can a Shark Detect a Heartbeat Through Solid Sand? Yes. Sharks' ampullae of Lorenzini — sensory pores covering their snouts — detect electrical fields as weak as 5 billionths of a volt per centimeter. A flatfish buried beneath sand produces enough field from muscle contractions alone for a passing shark to locate and strike it. (Source: Journal of Experimental Biology, 1971)

☑ How Does the Platypus Hunt Underwater With Its Eyes Closed? The platypus hunts with eyes, ears, and nostrils sealed shut. Its bill contains approximately 40,000 electroreceptors and 60,000 mechanoreceptors, detecting electrical fields and pressure changes from the muscle contractions of shrimp and fish. Every movement a prey animal makes betrays its precise location electrically. (Source: Journal of Experimental Biology, 1999)

☑ Can a Fish "See" Using Electricity? Weakly electric fish, such as the African elephantfish, generate a low-voltage field around their bodies. Objects distort this field in detectable ways, letting them sense shape, size, and conductivity without light. They navigate and hunt by electrical mapping as effectively in total darkness as in daylight. (Source: Science, 1996)

☑ **Can an Electric Eel Stun a Horse?** Electric eels generate discharges of up to 860 volts — powerful enough to stun a horse mid-leap. Kenneth Catania's research at Vanderbilt University demonstrated that when threatened by large animals, eels launch partially out of the water and press their chins against the threat, delivering an escalating shock directly to exposed flesh. Their weaker pulses serve navigation and electrolocation; the high-voltage burst remotely triggers involuntary muscle contractions in prey, immobilizing them before the eel strikes. (Source: Vanderbilt University, 2014)

☑ **How Do Pit Vipers Hunt in Complete Darkness?** Pit organs on vipers and pythons detect temperature differences as small as 0.003 degrees C. The thermal image is processed by the same brain region that handles vision, creating a heat overlay on normal sight. A warm mouse is detectable from 35 centimeters in total darkness. (Source: Nature, 2010)

☑ **How Do Vampire Bats Find Blood Vessels Through Fur?** Vampire bats have heat-sensing pit organs in their nose leaves that detect infrared radiation, pinpointing blood vessels within millimeters through fur or feathers. The neural pathway is distinct from all other known thermosensory systems — an independent solution to sensing heat found nowhere else among mammals. (Source: Nature, 2011)

☑ **Which Insect Actively Seeks Out Forest Fires?** The jewel beetle Melanophila acuminata has infrared-sensing pit organs on its thorax that detect fires from up to 50 miles (80 km) away. It flies toward the flames to lay eggs in freshly charred wood — the only insect known to deliberately navigate toward burning forests deliberately. (Source: Journal of Comparative Physiology A, 1998)

☑ **Do Sharks Have a Sixth Sense Beyond Electroreception?** Beyond their ampullae of Lorenzini, sharks possess a trigeminal system that detects pressure changes in the water column. This allows them to sense the bow wave produced by a swimming animal from dozens of meters away — registering the presence of prey before any electrical signal becomes detectable. (Source: Journal of Comparative Physiology A, 2000)

☑ **How Do Fish Sense Predators Approaching from Meters Away?** The lateral line — a row of fluid-filled canals running along a fish's flanks — detects pressure changes and water movements with extreme sensitivity. Fish use it to sense approaching predators, coordinate schooling behavior, and detect stationary objects by the distortions they create in water flow. (Source: Journal of Experimental Biology, 2002)

☑ **How Sensitive Is a Crocodile's Skin?** Dome pressure receptors covering a crocodile's entire jaw and body surface detect the impact of a single water drop from meters away. This allows crocodilians to identify the location, size, and movement pattern of an animal entering the water — purely from surface disturbances, in complete darkness. (Source: Integrative and Comparative Biology, 2002)

☑ **Can a Seal Track Fish by Their Wake Alone?** Harbor seals follow the hydrodynamic trail of a fish for up to 35 seconds after it has passed. Their whiskers (vibrissae) contain up to ten times more nerve endings than land mammal whiskers — sensitive enough to track a fish's wake through darkness and murky water. (Source: Journal of Experimental Biology, 2001)

☑ **How Do Jumping Spiders See in Almost Every Direction at Once?** Jumping spiders have eight eyes providing near-360-degree coverage. Two large forward-facing eyes deliver sharp color vision. Six smaller eyes detect peripheral motion. Together they give visual acuity rivaling insects 100 times their body size — all packed into a head barely two millimeters wide. (Source: Journal of Experimental Biology, 2007)

☑ **Why Can Eagles Spot Prey From Over a Mile Away?** Eagles and falcons have two foveas per eye — one for forward focus, one for lateral scanning. This dual system means a peregrine falcon at cruising altitude can spot a pigeon 1.8 miles (2.9 km) away while simultaneously monitoring for threats from the side. (Source: Journal of Comparative Physiology A, 2001)

☑ **How Do Horses Monitor Predators in Every Direction While Grazing?** Horses' laterally placed eyes provide a visual field approaching 350 degrees. Only two blind spots exist: directly ahead of the nose and directly behind the tail. This near-panoramic vision evolved to detect predators from any direction while the head is lowered in grazing. (Source: Applied Animal Behavior Science, 2010)

☑ **Why Do Insects Seem Impossible to Swat?** Insect compound eyes detect flickering at up to 300 cycles per second — five times faster than human eyes, which resolve about 60. A descending hand appears in slow motion to a fly. This visual processing speed gives insects a decisive edge in detecting and evading fast-moving threats. (Source: Journal of Experimental Biology, 1990)

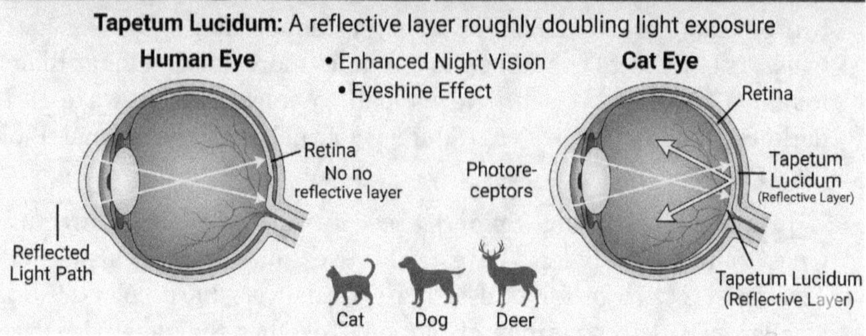

☑ **Why Do Animal Eyes Glow in the Dark?** A reflective layer called the tapetum lucidum sits behind the retina and bounces light back through the photoreceptors a second time, roughly doubling light exposure. Cats, dogs, and deer all possess it. The eyeshine in photographs is this layer reflecting the camera's flash at the lens. (Source: Veterinary Ophthalmology, 2003)

☑ **How Many Colors Can a Mantis Shrimp See?** Mantis shrimp have 16 types of photoreceptors versus three in humans. Yet research shows they don't see more colors — they identify wavelengths instantly without comparison, trading richness for speed. It is a sensory system built for rapid hunting decisions, not colorful experiences. (Source: Science, 2014)

☑ **How Can a Colorblind Animal Detect Color?** Octopuses have only one photoreceptor type — technically colorblind. Yet researchers propose their strangely shaped pupils may exploit chromatic aberration: different wavelengths focus at different depths, conveying color information. If confirmed, it would represent a sensory mechanism unlike anything else in the animal kingdom. (Source: PNAS, 2016)

☑ Why Do Bees See Flowers Differently From Humans? Bees detect ultraviolet light invisible to humans. Flower petals that appear plain to us display vivid bull's-eye patterns under UV — guides pointing directly to the nectar. From a bee's perspective, a plain white flower is an intricately patterned landing pad with a clearly marked center. (Source: Journal of Experimental Biology, 1994)

☑ Why Do Reindeer See in Ultraviolet Light? Reindeer have UV-sensitive vision, allowing them to see wolves against snow. Wolf fur absorbs UV light while snow reflects it, making wolves highly visible in UV even when they appear to blend into the landscape in normal visible light. (Source: Journal of Experimental Biology, 2011)

☑ Do Chameleons Have a Secret Signal Invisible to Predators? Many chameleon species display fluorescent patterns on their crests that glow brightly under ultraviolet light but are invisible in normal visible light. These UV patterns function as private communication channels for intraspecies signaling — entirely undetectable by predators that lack UV-sensitive vision. (Source: Nature, 2018)

☑ Do Catsharks Communicate Through a Hidden Visual Channel? Catsharks detect biofluorescent patterns on each other that glow green in blue ocean light — patterns invisible to most other fish. This gives them a private visual channel: catsharks can recognize and signal to one another using light that their predators and prey simply cannot see. (Source: Scientific Reports, 2019)

☑ How Do Birds of Paradise Produce Colors No Pigment Can Make? Several birds of paradise have feathers with nanostructures that manipulate light at the wavelength level, creating colors far more vivid than any pigment. Some species produce blacks absorbing 99.95% of all light, making adjacent colored plumage appear to glow brilliantly by contrast. (Source: Nature Communications, 2018)

☑ What Is Polarized Light — and Which Animals See It? Light waves oscillating on a single plane are invisible to humans but detectable by mantis shrimp, cuttlefish, and some insects. Cuttlefish display polarized patterns on their skin to communicate with each other — signals entirely invisible to fish predators that can see color perfectly. (Source: Current Biology, 2003)

☑ Do Dogs Really Smell in 3D? Dogs have up to 300 million olfactory receptors versus six million in humans. Their two nostrils work independently, sampling scent from slightly different positions. This directional sniffing triangulates a scent source the way stereo hearing locates sound — a spatial sense of smell humans have no equivalent for. (Source: Science, 2013)

☑ How Does a Salmon Find Its Birth Stream After Years at Sea? Pacific salmon imprint on their birth stream's unique chemical signature as juveniles. Years later, they detect specific amino acids and mineral combinations with extraordinary precision — locating a single stream among thousands by scent alone across thousands of miles of open ocean. (Source: Science, 1978)

☑ Why Do Snakes Flick Their Tongues Constantly? Snakes collect scent particles on their forked tongues and transfer them to the Jacobson's organ in the roof of the mouth. Each fork tip samples from a slightly different position — a higher concentration on one side pinpoints the direction of prey. (Source: Chemical Senses, 2002)

☑ Which Animal Has Taste Buds All Over Its Body? Channel catfish have approximately 175,000 taste buds distributed across their entire body surface, including fins and tail. As they swim, they taste the water passing over them, detecting prey chemically before they see or smell it. Every inch of their skin is, effectively, a tongue. (Source: PNAS, 1992)

☑ How Do Animals Navigate Without GPS or Maps? Loggerhead sea turtles detect both the inclination and intensity of Earth's magnetic field, pinpointing their geographic position with map-like precision. Homing pigeons use magnetite crystals in their beaks as a compass. Both animals navigate thousands of miles using a sense humans lack any equivalent of. (Source: Science, 2001)

☑ How Do Bees Navigate Inside a Dark Hive? Honeybees contain magnetite particles in their abdomens and use Earth's magnetic field to calibrate their waggle dance direction in total darkness. When researchers neutralize these particles experimentally, the dances become randomly disordered. Magnetic sense is the compass underpinning one of nature's most sophisticated navigational signals. (Source: Journal of Experimental Biology, 1989)

☑ Do Birds Literally See Earth's Magnetic Field? Cryptochrome proteins in birds' retinas react to magnetic fields, potentially appearing as light or shadow overlaid on normal vision. Robins and migratory birds may not sense north as an abstract feeling — they may see it as a visual pattern superimposed on the landscape ahead of them. (Source: Nature, 2004)

☑ **How Do Eels Navigate Across the Atlantic Ocean?** American eels hatch in the Sargasso Sea and navigate to rivers across North America using Earth's magnetic field, then return to reproduce. Experiments show they orient by both magnetic intensity and inclination — effectively reading a precise geographic position across thousands of ocean miles without any instruments. (Source: Current Biology, 2017)

☑ **Are Some Birds Born With a Built-In Star Map?** Young robins and warblers calibrate their magnetic sense by watching the rotation point of the night sky during their first weeks of life. This celestial reference becomes a lifelong navigational anchor. Deny them open-sky access as fledglings, and their ability to navigate correctly is permanently compromised. (Source: Science, 1996)

☑ **How Do Deep-Sea Fish Hunt in Total Darkness?** Below 3,300 feet (1,000 m), roughly 90% of creatures produce bioluminescence. The dragonfish Malacosteus niger evolved eyes sensitive to far-red light invisible to other deep-sea species — effectively hunting under a private searchlight. Its prey cannot see the beam being used to locate them. (Source: Science, 1998)

☑ **How Does a Barn Owl Strike Prey in Complete Darkness?** A barn owl's ear canals are positioned asymmetrically — one higher than the other — creating three-dimensional hearing accurate to within one degree. It can locate and strike a mouse moving beneath snow in total darkness, guided purely by sound. (Source: Science, 1981)

☑ **What Colors Can Sea Turtles See That Humans Cannot?** Sea turtles have four types of photoreceptors, including ultraviolet-sensitive cells, giving them color vision tuned to the underwater light spectrum. They detect UV light invisible to humans, likely aiding prey detection, navigation by underwater landmarks, and orientation using sky polarization patterns. (Source: Vision Research, 2005)

☑ **How Did Moths Evolve to Escape Bats?** Many moth species have ears tuned to bat echolocation frequencies. On detecting an approaching bat's biosonar, they immediately stop flapping and drop in a spiral dive — exploiting a gap in bat tracking. It is a sensory arms race, with bat sonar and moth hearing in continuous escalation. (Source: Journal of Experimental Biology, 1988)

The Language of Animals

☑ How Does a Bee Tell Her Colony Exactly Where to Find Flowers? The honeybee waggle dance encodes a food source's direction, distance, and quality in a single performance. The dance angle mirrors the sun's bearing; run duration indicates distance. Karl von Frisch decoded the system in the 1940s, earning a Nobel Prize for proving that an insect can transmit precise symbolic geographic information. (Source: Nobel Prize Committee, 1973)

☑ Can Prairie Dogs Describe a Predator's Color, Shape, and Size in a Single Bark? Dr. Con Slobodikoff at Northern Arizona University found that black-tailed prairie dog alarm calls encode descriptors for a predator's size, shape, color, and movement speed. The same colony produces different calls for a tall man in a blue shirt versus a short man in yellow — noun-adjective-like encoding in a single bark. (Source: Animal Cognition, 2009)

☑ Do Dolphins Have Individual Names for One Another? Every bottlenose dolphin develops a unique signature whistle within its first year — a personal acoustic label used throughout life. Dolphins mimic specific individuals' signature whistles to address them directly and will respond to their own name played back years later. It is the only confirmed non-human use of individual naming. (Source: PNAS, 2013)

☑ Do Vervet Monkeys Have Separate 'Words' for Eagle, Snake, and Leopard? Vervet monkeys produce three structurally distinct alarm calls — one for eagles, one for snakes, and one for leopards. Each triggers a different survival response: the eagle call sends vervets diving into bushes; the snake call makes them stand upright and scan the ground; the leopard call sends them into the highest branches. (Source: Animal Behavior, 1980)

☑ Did a Parrot Prove That Birds Can Truly Understand Concepts — Not Just Imitate Sounds? Alex, an African Grey parrot studied by Dr. Irene Pepperberg at Harvard, could identify 50 objects, seven colors, and five shapes. He grasped the concept of zero, asked questions spontaneously, and on the evening before his unexpected death in 2007, reportedly told Pepperberg, "You be good. I love you." (Source: Journal of Comparative Psychology, 2006)

☑ Did Cats Evolve a Special Vocalization Specifically to Manipulate Humans? Domestic cats produce a "solicitation purr" — a standard purr with a high-frequency cry embedded within it, matching the acoustic frequency of a human infant's distress call. Cats use this vocalization only with humans, never with each other. It evolved during domestication as a precision tool for triggering the human caregiving response. (Source: Current Biology, 2009)

☑ Can a Firefly Use Bioluminescent Flashing to Lure Members of Another Species to Their Death? Each firefly species has a species-specific flash pattern — a timed light code for finding mates in darkness. Female fireflies of the genus Photuris mimic the flash responses of other species, luring males of those species close, then eating them. It is one of the most precisely documented examples of deceptive interspecies communication in nature. (Source: Science, 1965)

☑ Can a Cuttlefish Show Two Completely Different Messages on Each Side of Its Body at the Same Time? Yes. A male cuttlefish caught between a rival male and a receptive female can display a female-mimicking pattern on his left side while showing aggressive male coloration on his right — simultaneously managing two conversations with two audiences. Chromatophores under independent neural control make each half of the skin a separate broadcast channel. (Source: Current Biology, 2012)

☑ Do Ravens Use Gestures to Share Information — the Way Humans and Great Apes Do? Ravens have been documented using their beaks to gesture toward objects — directing a partner's gaze toward food, a threat, or a location. This referential pointing was once considered unique to humans and great apes. Its presence in ravens suggests the behavior evolved independently at least twice, driven by the social demands of cooperative life. (Source: Nature Communications, 2011)

☑ Are Humpback Whales Composing and Sharing Music Across Entire Ocean Basins? Humpback whale songs follow a structured sequence of phrases and themes lasting up to 20 hours. Males across entire ocean basins share the same song — and songs evolve gradually, with new variants spreading westward across the Pacific. The phenomenon is cultural transmission on an oceanic scale, driven purely by imitation. (Source: Science, 2011)

☑ How Do Elephants Hold Conversations Across Miles of Savanna? Elephants produce rumbles at 14–35 Hz — well below the 20 Hz lower limit of human hearing. These infrasonic calls travel through the air across great distances. A family herd can receive and respond to a contact call from over 6 miles (10 km) away, coordinating movements without producing any sound audible to humans. (Source: Elephant Voices Project, 1994)

☑ Can Elephants Communicate Through the Ground Beneath Their Feet? Elephants generate infrasonic vibrations that travel as seismic waves through soil. Fat pads in their feet and lower jaw transmit these ground pulses to the inner ear. Field studies confirmed herds detecting and orienting toward seismic calls from other elephants more than 20 miles (32 km) away, even in the complete absence of airborne sound. (Source: Journal of the Acoustical Society of America, 2001)

☑ Do Sperm Whale Families Have Their Own Cultural Dialects Passed Down Through Generations? Sperm whales communicate using rapid click sequences called codas. Different family clans within the same ocean use distinctly different coda patterns, and these dialects are learned rather than inherited — passed from mother to calf. Whales born into one clan adopt its dialect; contact with other clans does not erase these learned differences. (Source: Animal Behavior, 2016)

☑ Do Different Orca Pods Speak Mutually Incomprehensible Dialects? Orca pods maintain distinct vocal repertoires of clicks and calls, passed from mother to calf. Over a dozen separate dialects have been identified among North Pacific killer whales — acoustically as different from each other as separate languages. Pods sharing a dialect form social clans; those with incompatible dialects rarely interact, even in the same waters. (Source: Animal Behavior, 1998)

☑ Do Humpback Whale Song Trends Sweep Across the Pacific Like Hit Songs? When a new humpback whale song variant appears in one population, it can spread across an entire ocean basin within two years — replacing earlier versions entirely. Researchers documented this cultural sweep moving westward from Australia into French Polynesia and then to Hawaii, traveling thousands of miles without any physical contact between singers. (Source: Current Biology, 2011)

☑ Can a Plant Send a Chemical Signal That Summons the Natural Predators of Its Attackers? When caterpillars attack corn plants, the plants release airborne volatile compounds that attract parasitoid wasps — the caterpillars' natural predators. The plant effectively broadcasts a chemical distress call that recruits defenders it cannot produce or move itself. This indirect defense strategy has been documented in over 50 plant species worldwide. (Source: Science, 1990)

☑ How Do Ants Encode Multiple Distinct Messages in a Single Chemical Trail? Leafcutter ants use over a dozen distinct pheromone compounds in their foraging trails. Different compounds signal "food found," "danger ahead," "follow this route," or "trail abandoned." Concentration further modifies meaning — a faint alarm compound means mild danger; a strong burst means evacuate immediately. This layered chemical vocabulary has no equivalent in the insect world. (Source: Journal of Chemical Ecology, 2003)

☑ Can an Ant Signal Its Own Death as a Chemical Message to Its Colony? When a honeybee or ant dies, its body releases oleic acid — a compound colony members recognize as a death signal. Workers carry the corpse to a designated refuse area. When scientists painted oleic acid onto living ants, nestmates repeatedly attempted to carry them out of the nest, regardless of the painted ant's struggling. (Source: Journal of Insect Physiology, 1959)

☑ How Does a Male Spider Court a Female Without Making a Single Audible Sound? Male orb-weaving spiders pluck specific strands of a female's web to produce vibrational signals she can recognize as courtship. Frequency, rhythm, and amplitude together encode species identity and fitness. Females distinguish deliberate courtship plucking from the random vibrations of trapped prey — responding to one with stillness and the other with an attack. (Source: Animal Behavior, 1997)

☑ Do Blind Underground Mole Rats Communicate by Headbanging? Cape mole rats communicate in sealed burrow systems by drumming their heads against the tunnel ceiling, producing seismic pulses that travel through soil to neighboring burrows. Different drumming rates encode distinct territorial and social messages. Each individual's drum pattern is individually recognizable — a seismic signature as distinct as a fingerprint. (Source: Journal of Zoology, 1990)

☑ How Do Termites Raise a Colony-Wide Alarm Without Any Sound Humans Can Detect? Termite soldiers signal a nest breach by drumming their heads against tunnel walls up to 11 times per second, producing seismic pulses that spread through the nest structure. Workers throughout the colony respond by sealing tunnels before the threat arrives — defense mobilized entirely through vibration, without a single airborne sound. (Source: Insectes Sociaux, 1998)

☑ Do Some Birds Follow Grammatical Rules When Composing Their Songs? Bengalese finches arrange song elements according to fixed syntactic rules, inserting specific note types only in particular positions — much like sentence structure in language. Researchers at Kyoto University demonstrated that finches react differently to syntactically "incorrect" sequences, suggesting a basic form of grammar predates its appearance in human language by millions of years. (Source: Nature Neuroscience, 2011)

☑ Do Different Bird Species Understand Each Other's Alarm Calls? Research published in 2021 found that Australian superb fairy-wrens accurately recognize and respond to the alarm calls of completely unrelated honeyeater species — birds with entirely different evolutionary histories and song traditions. This cross-species alarm comprehension appears to operate across multiple unrelated bird families, indicating shared communication systems far more widespread than scientists previously believed. (Source: Current Biology, 2021)

☑ Can a Wolf Recognize Which Pack Member Is Calling — From Their Howl Alone? Wolves encode individual identity in their howls through unique combinations of harmonic structure and frequency modulation. Field playback experiments showed that wolf packs respond differently to familiar packmates' howls versus those of strangers — approaching familiar calls and showing territorial avoidance toward unknown ones. A wolf can be identified by voice alone across miles of wilderness. (Source: Animal Behavior, 2014)

☑ Can Chimpanzees Identify Specific Individuals by Voice From Half a Mile Away? Chimpanzees produce a distinctive long-distance vocalization called the pant-hoot, with an acoustic structure unique to each individual. Field playback experiments showed that other chimpanzees accurately identified the caller from up to 0.6 miles (1 km) away, responding differently to the voices of familiar group members versus strangers without any visual contact. (Source: Animal Behavior, 1992)

☑ How Large Is a Wild Chimpanzee's Gestural Vocabulary? Researchers studying multiple wild chimpanzee populations identified 66 distinct gestures with consistent, agreed-upon meanings shared across populations — a genuine gestural vocabulary. Many of these gestures spontaneously overlap with those produced by human infants, suggesting a shared gestural foundation that predates the human-chimpanzee split by millions of years. (Source: Current Biology, 2014)

☑ Do Gibbons Compose Original Songs as a Mated Pair — Unique to Each Couple? Gibbon pairs perform coordinated vocal duets with call-and-response sequences unique to each mating pair. Males and females exchange calls in precisely timed acoustic alternation, creating a joint performance that reinforces their pair bond and defends territory. No two pairs produce the same duet — the song is an emergent expression of their specific partnership. (Source: Bioacoustics, 2004)

☑ Does the Naked Mole Rat Queen Literally Train Her Workers to Speak Like Her? Naked mole rat queens produce distinctive chirps that colony workers gradually learn to mimic. Members recognize each other partly by shared vocal dialect. When a queen dies and is replaced, the successor's calls progressively shift to match the new queen's pattern — the workers reprogram their own vocalizations to remain aligned with their new leader. (Source: Science, 2021)

☑ How Does a Colorblind Animal Produce Such Vivid Visual Signals? Octopuses are entirely colorblind — yet they create elaborate, rapidly shifting color patterns across their skin using chromatophores and iridophores under direct neural control. These displays signal aggression, submission, and species recognition. Scientists believe octopuses may interpret these patterns through polarized light sensitivity, reading signals invisible in color but distinct in polarization angle. (Source: Current Biology, 2015)

☑ Are Frog Calls Acoustic Barriers That Prevent Different Species From Interbreeding? Each frog species produces calls with species-specific frequency, pulse rate, and temporal structure. Females reject calls that deviate from their species' exact acoustic template. Where two related species overlap geographically, their calls diverge further apart than in zones where they do not — a phenomenon called acoustic character displacement, preventing hybridization through sound. (Source: Evolution, 1989)

☑ Is the Ocean Full of Animal Voices We Cannot Hear From the Surface? Hundreds of fish species produce sounds using muscles drumming against their swim bladders, or by grinding gill teeth. The oyster toadfish produces loud boatwhistle calls at dusk to attract mates; weakfish drum to coordinate spawning. The ocean is acoustically complex — fish were communicating through sound for hundreds of millions of years before humans ever listened. (Source: Bioacoustics, 2002)

☑ Can You Measure the Temperature by Counting Cricket Chirps? Yes — with surprising precision. The snowy tree cricket chirps faster as the temperature rises, following a formula called Dolbear's Law: count chirps in 14 seconds and add 40 to get the approximate temperature in degrees Fahrenheit. Published in 1897, the formula remains accurate enough for use as a field thermometer today. (Source: The American Naturalist, 1897)

☑ Can a Wild Bird Accurately Reproduce the Sound of a Chainsaw? The superb lyrebird of Australia has the most complex vocal apparatus of any songbird and learns sounds from its environment with remarkable accuracy — including camera shutters, chainsaws, and even mobile phone ringtones heard in forests. Male lyrebirds incorporate these environmental sounds into courtship displays, building a repertoire that signals their local experience to potential mates. (Source: Current Biology, 2013)

☑ Does the Gorilla's Famous Chest Beat Actually Encode Factual Information About Its Size? Male gorillas beat their chests with cupped hands, producing sounds audible up to 0.6 miles (1 km) through dense forest. Research found that peak frequencies in the chest-beat accurately encode the male's body size — allowing rival males to assess an opponent's physical capability at a distance, without risking confrontation. (Source: Scientific Reports, 2021)

☑ Are City Birds Evolving New Songs to Be Heard Over Urban Traffic? Great tits in European cities produce songs at higher frequencies than their rural counterparts — an adaptation to urban traffic noise, which masks lower-frequency sounds. The shift occurred within a few decades and is proportional to local noise levels. It is one of the fastest documented cases of acoustic adaptation to a human-altered environment. (Source: Nature, 2006)

☑ Do Young Songbirds Have a Limited Window to Learn Their Species' Song — and What Happens If They Miss It? Zebra finches and most songbirds undergo a critical vocal-learning period in their first 90 days of life. During this window, they memorize a song template from their father and later reproduce it. Birds deprived of a model during this period develop permanently abnormal vocalizations that cannot be corrected by later exposure. (Source: Science, 1990)

☑ Do Ground Squirrels Sound Different Alarms for Different Levels of Danger? California ground squirrels produce acoustically distinct calls based on predator type, proximity, and threat level. A terrestrial predator triggers a different call from an aerial one; a close predator triggers a more urgent variant. Listeners respond proportionately — diving into burrows for high-urgency calls and merely standing alert for lower-urgency warnings. (Source: Behavioral Ecology, 1995)

☑ Why Does the Nightingale Sound Like a Different Bird Every Time It Sings? A male nightingale possesses a repertoire of up to 200 distinct song types, cycling through them during a single performance lasting hours. Males with larger repertoires attract mates more successfully — the size of a male's song collection serving as an honest signal of age, survival experience, and genetic quality that females evaluate directly. (Source: Animal Behavior, 1981)

☑ Do Honeybees From Different Countries Dance in Different Dialects? European and Asian honeybee subspecies encode distance at different rates in their waggle dances: the same dance-run duration signals different distances to each population. When researchers created mixed-subspecies colonies, bees consistently misread each other's dances, sending foragers to the wrong locations. The waggle dance has geographic dialects, just as human languages do. (Source: PNAS, 2008)

☑ Do Alligators Broadcast Their Calls Through the Water's Surface in a Visible Display? During bellowing, American alligators produce infrasonic vibrations at around 10–20 Hz that cause the water surface directly above them to "dance" in an arc of rising droplets — a phenomenon sometimes called the "water dance." Sound and vibration are broadcast simultaneously to rivals and mates, combining acoustic and tactile channels in one display. (Source: Copeia, 2000)

Hunters and the Hunted

☑ How Does a Cheetah Reach 70 mph Without Its Body Tearing Itself Apart? The cheetah achieves 70 mph (113 km/h) not through muscle power alone, but through a uniquely flexible spine that functions as a compression spring. At full gallop, the spine contracts and extends with each stride, adding approximately five feet (1.5 m) of additional reach per cycle. Unlike other big cats, its claws are semi-retractable, gripping the ground like cleats rather than serving as weapons. Each complete stride covers up to 23 feet (7 m), and the cheetah can accelerate from zero to 60 mph (97 km/h) in under three seconds. (Source: Royal Veterinary College, 2013)

☑ Why Does the World's Fastest Land Animal Lose Its Prey More Often Than Most People Assume? Despite reaching 70 mph (113 km/h), the cheetah is a pure sprinting specialist with almost no aerobic reserve. A chase exceeding 30 seconds risks fatal overheating — body temperature can approach 105 degrees F (41 degrees C) within a minute of all-out effort. After a successful kill, the cheetah must rest for up to 30 minutes before eating, during which lions, hyenas, and even vultures frequently steal the carcass. In open savanna studies, cheetahs lose up to 50% of their kills to larger scavengers before they can consume them. (Source: Royal Veterinary College, 2013)

☑ Why Is the Dragonfly the Most Lethally Accurate Predator Ever Studied? Dragonflies achieve a hunting success rate of approximately 95% — the highest of any predator on record. Lions succeed roughly 25% of the time; great white sharks, around 55%. The dragonfly's advantage is entirely predictive: rather than chasing prey reactively, it calculates its target's trajectory and flies directly to where the prey will be, intercepting it in mid-air. Research confirmed the dragonfly executes this ballistic interception using as few as three to four neurons — performing real-time targeting calculations faster than any engineering system humans have built at equivalent scale. (Source: Nature, 2015)

☑ How Does a Peregrine Falcon Survive a Dive at 240 mph Without Its Lungs Rupturing? The peregrine falcon enters its hunting stoop at up to 240 mph (386 km/h) — the fastest recorded movement of any animal. To prevent lung damage from the pressure of incoming air, a bony tubercle inside each nostril deflects airflow into a spiral, slowing pressure at the point of intake. A nictitating membrane clears debris from the eyes at speed. At the moment of impact, the falcon strikes with a partly closed talon rather than gripping, transferring lethal kinetic energy to prey while eliminating the risk of a broken leg in a full-speed collision. (Source: National Geographic)

☑ What Mathematical Formula Does a Peregrine Falcon Solve Entirely in Its Own Brain During a Dive? Rather than plunging straight at its target, a peregrine follows a logarithmic spiral — the same curve used in guided missile systems — keeping prey at a fixed angle in its visual field throughout the stoop. This approach maximizes target visibility while minimizing aerodynamic drag from turning at speed. Computer modeling confirmed this strategy, revealing the bird performs real-time ballistic calculations during a fall at 240 mph (386 km/h) — the same mathematics that missile engineers formalized decades later — through neural processing operating in fractions of a second. (Source: Journal of Experimental Biology, 2000)

☑ How Does a Spider That Cannot See Its Prey Know the Exact Moment to Strike? The trapdoor spider lives inside a silk-lined burrow sealed by a hinged lid of earth and silk. Silk trip lines radiate outward across the surrounding ground. When an insect contacts a line, the vibration travels to the spider's legs within milliseconds. Studies show the spider identifies which tripwire was triggered, gauges the prey's size from vibration amplitude, and positions itself behind the door before it opens. The entire sequence — vibration detection, target assessment, and strike — is completed in under 50 milliseconds, faster than a human blink. (Source: Journal of Zoology, 1998)

☑ Can a Shrimp's Claw Briefly Approach the Temperature of the Sun's Surface? When the pistol shrimp snaps its enlarged claw shut, the resulting jet of water moves so fast it generates a collapsing cavitation bubble in its wake. As the bubble implodes, it releases a pressure wave registering 189 dB — louder than a gunshot at close range — and a flash of light and heat briefly approaching 9,000 degrees F (5,000 degrees C), close to the temperature of the Sun's photosphere. The prey is stunned or killed before the shrimp has physically made contact. The claw is not the weapon. The collapsing water is. (Source: Nature, 2000)

☑ How Do Orcas Use Waves as a Precision Weapon to Hunt Seals on Antarctic Ice? Orcas in Antarctic waters have developed a cooperative hunting technique based on physics rather than force. A coordinated group lines up and charges toward an ice floe in formation, generating a targeted wave. The wave washes a seal cleanly off the ice and into the water, where waiting pod members catch it. This technique is not instinctive — it is culturally learned and transmitted, being taught from mother to calf across multiple generations. Different orca populations have developed distinct regional variants of the same basic cooperative wave strategy. (Source: Marine Mammal Science, 2006)

☑ What Is the Spinning Vortex Trap That Norwegian Orcas Use to Harvest Entire Herring Schools? In Norwegian waters, orca pods use a technique called carousel feeding. Pod members encircle a herring school at speed while slapping the surface with their flukes, trapping the fish in a compressed ball near the surface. Individual orcas then charge through the ball with open mouths. The behavior requires precise coordination — every animal must time its movements relative to the others. Carousel feeding is regional: Norwegian orcas use it routinely; Icelandic orcas from the same species typically do not, confirming it as a culturally transmitted innovation rather than an instinctive behavior. (Source: Animal Behavior, 2007)

☑ Why Does the Great White Shark Attack Its Prey From Directly Below at Full Speed? Great white sharks hunting Cape fur seals near Cape Town, South Africa, use a near-vertical ambush from depth. The seal's silhouette against the bright surface sky is clearly visible from below, while the ascending shark, emerging from darkness, is invisible to the seal above. Strikes often propel the shark entirely clear of the water. Underwater camera research confirmed sharks select approach angles that maximize surprise, and they time strikes to moments when seal alertness is reduced — choosing ambush geometry with what researchers describe as consistent tactical precision. (Source: Journal of Zoology, 2001)

☑ Why Does a Great White Shark Sometimes Bite and Then Back Away From Its Own Prey? When great white sharks encounter large prey — particularly adult elephant seals capable of inflicting serious wounds with powerful flippers — they frequently deliver a single bite and withdraw to a safe distance before approaching again. Researchers have documented this behavior extensively, interpreting it as injury avoidance: the shark assesses the risk of a prolonged struggle against large, mobile prey and opts to wait. A wounded animal will eventually weaken without requiring the shark to remain within reach of a creature that can fight back with considerable force. (Source: Wildlife Research, 2005)

☑ How Does the Largest Animal on Earth Survive by Eating Some of the Smallest Creatures? The blue whale's jaw can expand to engulf a volume of water approaching its own body volume in a single lunge, taking in hundreds of thousands of gallons in seconds. Baleen plates — between 250 and 400 of them, made of keratin — act as sieves, straining millions of krill from the expelled water. A blue whale consumes up to eight tons (7.3 metric tons) of krill per day during peak Antarctic summer feeding — requiring astonishing quantities of the ocean's smallest prey to sustain the planet's largest body. (Source: NOAA Fisheries)

☑ What Hangs From a Deep-Sea Fish's Head and Uses Light It Didn't Produce to Attract Prey? The female anglerfish dangles a modified dorsal spine above her head like a fishing rod, tipped with a luminous lure called the esca. The light is not the fish's own — bioluminescent bacteria colonize the esca and generate the glow autonomously. In the absolute darkness below 3,300 feet (1,000 m), any visible light source attracts curious prey. The anglerfish does nothing but wait. When prey approaches within range, the strike occurs too fast to follow in slow-motion video replay — a passive lure followed by the fastest feeding motion the animal is capable of. (Source: Copeia, 2005)

☑ How Does a Fish Correct for an Optical Illusion Caused by Water and Still Hit a Moving Target on Land? The archerfish spits a jet of water at insects perched above the surface, but faces a fundamental optical problem: water and air refract light at different angles, making an insect appear to be in a position offset from where it actually is. The archerfish compensates for this distortion instinctively, aiming where the prey physically is rather than where it appears to be. It also predicts where a dislodged insect will land before it falls, repositioning itself beneath the correct landing point before the prey hits the water. (Source: PNAS, 2004)

☑ How Does a Bird Use Its Own Wingspan as a Shade Trap to Lure Fish Toward It? The black heron (Egretta ardesiaca) of sub-Saharan Africa extends both wings forward and hunches over the water, forming a canopy of shade above the surface with its own body. Fish instinctively seek shaded areas, interpreting them as protective cover, and cluster beneath the arch the heron has created. As they gather, the bird strikes down into its own shadow. The technique simultaneously removes surface glare for the heron's own vision, attracts prey into a predictable position, and conceals the hunting posture from approaching fish — solving three predation problems with a single posture. (Source: African Birds & Birding, 1999)

☑ **How Does a Plant Know the Difference Between a Raindrop and a Fly?** The Venus flytrap operates on an electrical counting system. A single touch of a trigger hair generates an electrical pulse, but the trap does not close. A second touch within approximately 20 seconds generates a second pulse — and the two together trigger closure. This two-signal protocol filters out false alarms from rain, falling debris, and accidental contact. The plant literally counts. Once prey is confirmed, additional movements by the struggling insect generate further signals that accelerate the trap's tightening and trigger the release of digestive enzymes — the plant responding intelligently to real-time prey behavior. (Source: Current Biology, 2007)

☑ **Why Would a Plant Evolve to Eat Animals?** Carnivorous plants evolved specifically in environments where soil nitrogen is severely limited — bogs, fens, wet rocky outcrops, and tropical cloud forest floors, where roots cannot extract adequate nutrition. Animal prey provide the nitrogen that soil denies them. Remarkably, this solution evolved independently in at least 13 separate plant lineages, producing entirely different trap architectures — the snap trap, the sticky pad, the pitcher, and the suction bladder — each evolved on different continents from unrelated ancestors facing the same problem. Carnivory in plants is one of evolution's most repeated inventions. (Source: Plant Biology, 2009)

☑ **Which Bird of Prey Discovered the Cooperative Hunting Strategy That Was Supposed to Belong Only to Mammals?** Harris's hawks are the only raptors documented hunting in coordinated social teams — a behavior otherwise observed in wolves, lions, and dolphins. Groups of three to six birds pursue a jackrabbit simultaneously from different angles, cutting off escape routes. When one bird tires, another takes over the chase. After a kill, the group feeds cooperatively rather than competing. Research links this behavior to the species' unusually prolonged family bonds, suggesting cooperative hunting in raptors became possible only where the social structure to support it already existed. (Source: The Auk, 1988)

☑ Which Pack Hunter Has a Success Rate That Leaves Every Other Large Predator Far Behind? African wild dogs (Lycaon pictus) succeed in approximately 80% of their hunts — compared to lions at roughly 25% and spotted hyenas at 25–30%. Their strategy relies on endurance rather than speed: they pursue prey at a sustained 37 mph (60 km/h) for up to three miles (5 km), waiting for exhaustion to do the work. During the chase, pack members coordinate direction changes using high-pitched twittering calls, maintaining real-time tactical communication across the pursuit. Fewer than 6,000 remain in the wild, making the most efficient large predator on Earth also among its most endangered. (Source: African Wildlife Foundation, 2015)

☑ Which Spider Hunts by Throwing Its Own Web Directly at Its Prey? The net-casting spider (Deinopis sp.) constructs a small rectangular web held between its front legs, then hurls it over passing prey, stretching it to several times its resting area on impact. Its forward-facing eyes are among the largest relative to body size of any spider on Earth — specialized for extreme sensitivity in near-total darkness. When light conditions prevent visual targeting, the spider switches to sensing ground vibrations through its legs and deploys the same throwing technique using a purely tactile trigger. Two independent sensory systems feed the identical hunting action, giving this ambush predator redundant targeting capability. (Source: Animal Behavior, 2018)

☑ **How Does One Spider Hunt Another by Sending Deceptive Messages Down Its Own Web?** Portia fimbriata, a jumping spider from tropical Australia and Asia, hunts web-building spiders by entering their webs and transmitting precisely crafted vibrations along the silk — mimicking the signals of trapped prey, a struggling mate, or the web's own owner moving about. When the resident spider approaches, Portia times its strike to coincide with gusts of wind that mask its movement. Researchers found Portia tests different vibration patterns in real time, abandoning failed signals and adjusting until an approach works — a trial-and-error cognitive strategy in an animal with a brain smaller than a sesame seed. (Source: Animal Behavior, 1996)

☑ **How Do Wolves Select One Animal From an Entire Herd Without a Signal Anyone Can See?** Wolves approaching prey — elk, bison, or moose — test individuals by triggering short pursuit bursts. Animals that hold their ground are abandoned immediately; those that flee at an uneven gait, fall behind, or show labored breathing become the target. Once selected, the pack pursues in relay — wolves rotate through the leading position while others recover their breath — sustaining the chase for up to 5 miles (8 km). No single wolf can outrun a healthy elk in a straight race. The pack's success depends entirely on reading which animal is already failing and maintaining relentless pressure until it can no longer continue. (Source: Journal of Wildlife Management, 2007)

☑ **What Happens When a Group of Humpback Whales Builds a Curtain of Bubbles Around a School of Fish?** Humpback whales (Megaptera novaeangliae) in Alaskan and Antarctic waters cooperate to construct a bubble net: one or more whales dive beneath a fish school and spiral upward while exhaling, releasing a rising curtain of bubbles. Fish refuse to cross the bubble barrier, compressing into a dense column in the center. A designated whale then emits a specific low-frequency feeding call, and the group lunges upward simultaneously with mouths open. Studies documented groups of up to 22 whales performing this technique, with specific individuals consistently taking the same functional role across multiple hunts. (Source: Animal Behavior, 2003)

☑ What Serves as Both a Lethal Weapon and an Emergency Catapult in One of Nature's Fastest-Moving Animals? Trap-jaw ants of the genus Odontomachus close their mandibles at 145 mph (233 km/h) — fast enough to stun or kill an insect on contact. The strike is not a direct muscle action but a spring-latch mechanism: energy builds in loaded jaw muscles and releases instantaneously when triggered. When threatened by predators larger than any prey they could hunt, trap-jaw ants redirect this same mechanism against the ground itself. Striking the surface at full force produces a recoil that launches the ant up to 15 inches (38 cm) horizontally and 3 inches (8 cm) vertically. The identical structure serves offense in one context and escape in another. (Source: PNAS, 2006)

☑ Why Is the Chameleon's Tongue Faster Than Any Direct Muscle Action Could Explain? The chameleon tongue is not powered by muscle contraction during its launch. Elastic collagen layers wrapped around a central bone store energy like a compressed spring, and when the bone recoils, they release it in a single burst — accelerating the tongue to approximately 60 mph (97 km/h) in under one hundredth of a second. The tongue extends up to twice the animal's own body length. A sticky tip coated with mucus up to 400 times more viscous than human saliva adheres to the target on contact. The entire strike and retraction are completed before the insect's nervous system can register that a threat existed. (Source: Royal Society, 2004)

☑ **What Erupts From the Ocean Floor to Seize Fish in the Dark — and Why Did Scientists Miss It for Years?** The bobbit worm (Eunice aphroditois) burrows into sandy seafloor sediment, leaving only its sensory antennae exposed. When vibrations signal a fish overhead, it erupts from the sand, seizing prey with scissor-sharp jaws capable of cleanly severing a fish in two. Specimens can reach 10 feet (3 m) in length, though most encounters involve animals between 3 and 4 feet (90–120 cm). Because it lives entirely beneath the substrate, bobbit worms evaded detection in many reef sites for years — fish disappearing inexplicably, coral showing overnight damage — until careful excavation revealed the buried predator responsible. (Source: Journal of Natural History, 2012)

☑ **Why Would an Insect Keep Its Host Alive While Consuming It From the Inside Out?** Female Cotesia glomerata wasps locate host caterpillars by following the chemical signals plants release when their leaves are actively being eaten. The female injects up to 80 eggs through the caterpillar's skin using her ovipositor. Larvae hatch internally and feed on non-essential tissues first, keeping the caterpillar alive and feeding for weeks while they grow. When mature, they chew exit holes through the host's skin and spin cocoons on its exterior. The caterpillar — still technically alive — reflexively thrashes at any animal approaching the cocoons, defending its own killers from further parasites until it can no longer move. (Source: Journal of Chemical Ecology, 2005)

☑ **Which Hawk Uses the One Bird Its Prey Has Already Learned to Ignore as Its Primary Hunting Disguise?** The zone-tailed hawk (Buteo albonotatus) of the American Southwest and Central America mimics the silhouette, coloration, and rocking flight of the turkey vulture — a species that small prey animals have learned to ignore because vultures eat only carrion. Zone-tailed hawks fly within vulture flocks, tipping and rocking in the same characteristic manner on shared thermals. Lizards, birds, and rodents that suppress escape responses at the sight of a vulture remain stationary as the hawk circles overhead. When it breaks from the flock and drops, the prey has stood unmoving while a predator circled. The disguise exploits the prey animal's own learned threat-recognition memory. (Source: The Auk, 2004)

☑ Why Does a Crocodile Spin Its Entire Body Violently After Clamping Down on Prey It Cannot Chew? A crocodile's jaws grip with a force of 3,700 psi (255 bar) — the highest bite force recorded for any living animal — but cannot move laterally to slice meat. Once large prey is seized, the crocodile rolls its entire body in rapid, repeated rotations, using its own mass to torque flesh from bone and disorient prey still capable of struggling. The death roll is a mechanical solution to a structural limitation: immovable jaws combined with a body massive enough to function as a twisting lever. Saltwater crocodiles sustain bite force throughout the roll without measurable muscular fatigue, applying continuous pressure from the moment of seizure. (Source: Journal of Zoology, 2012)

☑ How Does a Cuttlefish Freeze Its Prey in Place Before It Is Within Striking Range? Cuttlefish (Sepia sp.) hunting shrimp and small fish employ a behavior called the passing cloud display: a rapid wave of dark color bands flows across the animal's skin from front to back in continuous, rhythmic motion. High-speed camera analysis shows prey animals stop moving within seconds of the display beginning and remain stationary until the cuttlefish is within strike range. The mechanism is believed to exploit a freeze reflex in crustacean visual systems, where continuous moving patterns trigger immobility rather than flight. The cuttlefish adjusts the wave's speed and intensity based on the prey's responses, calibrating its display in real time. (Source: Journal of Experimental Biology, 2012)

☑ **Which Animal Has Evolved a Tongue That Looks Exactly Like a Living Worm and Uses It to Hunt?** The alligator snapping turtle (Macrochelys temminckii) of the American South holds the most patient ambush strategy of any freshwater reptile. It rests on the river bottom with its jaws open, motionless for hours, wiggling a bright pink, worm-shaped appendage attached to its tongue. Small fish interpret the movement as live prey and swim directly into the open mouth. The turtle requires no pursuit, no timing, and no energy beyond the tongue's gentle motion. With jaws strong enough to sever a human finger, the strike occurs the instant a fish contacts the lure. Captive specimens have held the same ambush posture for over an hour before a successful strike. (Source: Herpetologica, 2003)

☑ **What Does an Assassin Bug Do With the Bodies of Its Victims That Makes the Next Kill Easier?** The masked hunter (Reduvius personatus), a species of assassin bug native to North America and Europe, coats its nymph body with particles of debris and dust, and with the drained, empty husks of its ant prey. These accumulated corpses make the nymph visually indistinguishable from nest debris inside a leafcutter ant colony. Moving undetected among ants, it continues hunting further victims. The coating also functions as a contact irritant that discourages larger predators from investigating the insect. Each successful kill adds to the disguise, making the assassin bug progressively harder to detect as the hunt continues. (Source: Journal of Insect Behavior, 2010)

☑ **Why Did the Komodo Dragon's Real Kill Mechanism Go Undetected for Over 75 Years of Scientific Study?** For decades, Varanus komodoensis was believed to kill through bacterial infection spread by its notoriously septic saliva. In 2009, researchers demonstrated this was wrong on both counts: Komodo mouths carry no unusual concentration of dangerous bacteria, and infection alone cannot reliably kill large prey at the speed required. Dissection revealed venom glands between the lower jaw teeth, producing anticoagulants and compounds that drop blood pressure and induce shock in bitten animals. The bacteria myth had been accepted in zoology textbooks for over 75 years. The actual mechanism had already been confirmed in related monitor lizards — it was simply never looked for in the world's largest living lizard. (Source: PNAS, 2009)

☑ **How Does a Crustacean the Size of a Cigar Strike Hard Enough to Shatter Aquarium Glass — and What Are Engineers Learning From Its Fist?** The peacock mantis shrimp (Odontodactylus scyllarus) strikes with club-shaped appendages at 50 mph (80 km/h) — one of the fastest recorded limb movements of any animal. The impact generates a cavitation bubble at the point of contact, adding a second pressure wave to the initial blow. The club is constructed from hydroxyapatite fibers arranged in a helicoidal pattern that distributes stress across multiple layers rather than concentrating it at a fracture point, resisting thousands of full-force strikes without cracking. Materials engineers are actively modeling this structure for impact-resistant armor, vehicle panels, and protective helmets. (Source: Journal of Experimental Biology, 2011)

☑ **What Is "Kerplunking," and Why Do Only Some Bottlenose Dolphin Populations Know How to Do It?** Bottlenose dolphins in Shark Bay, Western Australia, use a culturally transmitted technique called kerplunking. One dolphin slaps a shallow mudflat with its tail flukes, releasing a rising column of mud and sediment that panics a school of mullet into a compressed ball near the surface. Other pod members wait at the perimeter and catch fish as they leap to escape. The behavior is learned, not instinctive — juveniles observe adults for months before performing it independently. Research confirmed kerplunking is practiced routinely in Shark Bay but is absent from dolphin populations in ecologically identical nearby waters, confirming cultural transmission rather than environmental necessity. (Source: Marine Mammal Science, 1997)

☑ **How Did the Tawny Frogmouth Turn Absolute Stillness Into a Complete Predation Strategy?** The tawny frogmouth (Podargus strigoides) of Australia neither pursues nor actively ambushes prey. By day, it perches motionless on a broken branch with plumage compressed, eyes slitted, and bill tilted upward, mimicking the texture and color of weathered wood with such precision that experienced birdwatchers have stood within arm's reach without detecting it. At night, it opens its wide, frog-like gape and waits. Insects and small vertebrates approach the dark cavity and enter it. There is no chase, no calculated strike, no cooperative coordination — only a bird that has perfected becoming invisible, then letting prey come to it. (Source: Emu: Austral Ornithology, 2003)

☑ **What Does a Starfish Do When It Catches a Mussel Too Large to Fit Through Its Own Mouth?** Sea stars possess no jaw, no teeth, and a mouth aperture only a few millimeters wide — yet routinely prey on mussels and clams sealed inside shells far larger than anything they could swallow. The solution is anatomically extraordinary: the starfish wraps its arms around the closed shell and sustains muscular tension for minutes or hours until the exhausted mussel relaxes and its shell gaps open by a fraction of a millimeter. Through this gap, the starfish pushes its own stomach outside its body and into the shell cavity, digesting the mussel's soft tissue externally before drawing the pre-liquefied meal back inside. Digestion occurs entirely outside the predator's body. (Source: Invertebrate Biology, 2009)

☑ Why Is a Mouse Incapable of Hearing the Predator That Has Already Pinpointed Its Location? The great horned owl (Bubo virginianus) approaches prey without generating detectable sound, due to three feather adaptations operating simultaneously. Comb-like serrations on leading-edge flight feathers break up airflow turbulence before it produces noise. A fringe on trailing-edge feathers smooths disrupted air behind the wing. A velvet-like surface coating on each feather vane absorbs residual sound rather than reflecting it. Wind-tunnel measurements confirm great horned owls produce sound at or below the ambient noise floor in quiet conditions — effectively inaudible to prey. The owl's asymmetrically positioned ears, meanwhile, triangulate the target's location with sub-centimeter precision before the approach begins. (Source: Journal of Experimental Biology, 2017)

☑ **Which Two Predators From Entirely Different Classes Cooperate to Hunt Using Signals They Appear to Have Developed Together?** In Red Sea and Indo-Pacific coral reefs, groupers and moray eels form hunting partnerships that cross class boundaries. A grouper hovering at the reef surface signals a resting moray eel by shaking its head rapidly — a gesture shown experimentally to communicate the location of prey hidden in a crevice. The eel enters the crevice and flushes the prey into open water, where the grouper intercepts it. Neither animal shares the catch. Researchers found groupers approach specific familiar individual morays and wait, demonstrating individual recognition across species — a cognitive demand previously associated only with primates and corvids, not fish. (Source: PLOS ONE, 2012)

☑ **When a School of Fish Is Attacked Simultaneously by Sharks, Dolphins, and Diving Seabirds, What Does It Become?** A bait ball forms when a fish school — sardines, anchovies, or herring — collapses inward under attack from multiple predators simultaneously. Each fish follows three simple rules: stay close to its neighbors, match their speed and direction, and move away from anything larger. The emergent result is a dense, spinning sphere that continuously cycles members from the exposed outer surface toward the protected interior. No individual fish directs the formation. Despite this, bait balls can persist for hours against simultaneous predation by sharks, dolphins, and plunge-diving gannets — each fish improving its statistical odds of survival simply by not being the one on the outside at any given moment. (Source: Behavioral Ecology, 2006)

☑ **Which Animal Can Impersonate More Than 15 Different Species on Demand?** The mimic octopus (Thaumoctopus mimicus) alters its shape, color, and movement to impersonate over 15 species — flatfish, lionfish, and banded sea snakes. Unlike animals that simply hide, it actively performs. Field researchers documented it selecting different impersonations based on which predator was approaching, suggesting contextual decision-making unknown in any other invertebrate. (Source: Proceedings of the Royal Society B, 2001)

☑ **How Do 500,000 Birds Move as a Single Body Without a Leader?** Starling murmurations operate on three rules per bird: match the speed and direction of your seven nearest neighbors, stay close, and avoid collision. No leader exists. Each response cascades through the flock faster than any individual predator can track a single bird, making individual targeting nearly impossible against a shape that never holds still. (Source: PNAS, 2008)

☑ What Happens Inside a Bombardier Beetle When a Predator Attacks? The bombardier beetle stores hydroquinone and hydrogen peroxide separately. Under threat, they combine in a catalytic chamber and fire as a 212°F (100°C) boiling chemical pulse through a rotating nozzle — up to 500 bursts per second, aimed in almost any direction. The spray is hot enough to injure or deter attacking predators outright. (Source: Journal of Experimental Biology, 1999)

☑ How Does a Caterpillar Impersonate a Snake Well Enough to Fool a Bird? The elephant hawk-moth caterpillar (Deilephila elpenor) retracts its head and inflates its front body segments when threatened, revealing large eyespots and forming a snake-head shape, then sways slowly. Studies confirmed birds abandon attacks at significantly higher rates than against non-mimicking caterpillars — the inflation triggering innate snake-avoidance even in birds with no prior snake experience. (Source: Proceedings of the Royal Society B, 2012)

☑ Why Can No Natural Predator Unroll a Pangolin? The pangolin's overlapping keratin scales deflect a lion's claws; no predator can bite through them. When threatened, it curls into a ball, protecting every soft surface. No animal can unroll it. Against human poachers, who simply lift it whole, the defense fails, making pangolins the most heavily trafficked mammal on Earth. (Source: African Wildlife Foundation, 2014)

☑ What Makes a Poison Dart Frog's Most Dangerous Feature Its Most Visible Trait? Poison dart frogs advertise their toxicity through vivid neon coloration rather than hiding — a strategy called aposematism. Any predator that survives contact learns permanently to avoid that color. The more lethal the species, the brighter its warning signal must be, since conspicuousness is only advantageous when backed by something genuinely dangerous. (Source: PNAS, 2005)

☑ Can a Lizard Shoot Blood From Its Eyes at a Predator? The Texas horned lizard restricts blood flow from its head until eye sinus vessels rupture, projecting a stream up to 5 feet (1.5 m). The blood contains compounds from harvester ants toxic to canid predators — coyotes and wolves — but harmless to raptors, making the defense chemically calibrated to the lizard's most dangerous threat. (Source: Copeia, 2001)

☑ Are Porcupine Quills More Dangerous After They Enter Skin Than at First Impact? North American porcupine quills carry microscopic backward-facing barbs. Once embedded, muscle contractions drive them deeper at approximately 1 mm per hour, making removal extremely difficult. The quills also carry antibiotic fatty acids on their surface, reducing infection in self-inflicted injuries. No other quilled animal is known to coat its defensive spines with antibiotics. (Source: PNAS, 2012)

☑ Which Salamander Uses Its Own Rib Cage as a Venomous Weapon? The Spanish ribbed newt (Pleurodeles waltl) pushes its ribs outward through its own skin when seized. As the ribs pierce through, they pass through toxic skin glands, coating themselves in venomous mucus. Any predator gripping the newt drives a row of self-poisoned spines into its own flesh. The punctures heal rapidly once the threat passes. (Source: Journal of Zoology, 2009)

☑ **Why Does the Horror Frog Deliberately Break Its Own Bones?** The hairy frog (Trichobatrachus robustus) of Central Africa, when seized, deliberately contracts muscles that snap its own toe bones. The fractured tips puncture through the skin, creating claws. No other vertebrate creates defensive weapons through deliberate self-fracture. Researchers believe the claws retract when muscles relax, though the healing mechanism remains only partially understood. (Source: Biology Letters, 2008)

☑ **How Does the Mimic Octopus Decide Which Species to Impersonate?** The mimic octopus does not cycle randomly through impersonations. When pursued by damselfish, it preferentially mimics the banded sea snake — which preys on damselfish — suggesting it identifies its attacker and selects the most threatening impersonation for that specific predator. This contextual decision-making implies predator recognition and behavioral memory unique among invertebrates. (Source: Coral Reefs, 2001)

☑ **What Makes the Satanic Leaf-Tailed Gecko Effectively Invisible Even to Trained Eyes?** The satanic leaf-tailed gecko (Uroplatus phantasticus) of Madagascar mimics a dead leaf in precise detail — frayed edges, brown mottling, and a flattened tail replicating decay. During daylight, it presses flat against bark, eliminating the shadow that betrays most resting animals. Field researchers have stepped directly over individuals without detecting them, even while actively searching. (Source: Copeia, 2008)

☑ **Is There an Insect So Well Camouflaged It Includes Fake Fungal Spots and Bite Marks?** Dead leaf mantids (Deroplatys species) replicate leaf color, shape, and surface details — including simulated bite marks and fungal decay blemishes. A predator scanning for living prey sees decomposing plant material instead. The camouflage defeats the predator's recognition system rather than its vision — the mantid is not hidden; it is reclassified as something inedible. (Source: Journal of Morphology, 2014)

☑ **How Does a Stick Insect Disguise Its Own Eggs?** Stick insects (Phasmatodea) match bark and twig color, texture, and surface profile. At rest, gentle body swaying mimics branch movement in a breeze. Their camouflage extends to eggs: Phasmatodea eggs resemble plant seeds so closely that ants carry them underground, inadvertently ensuring germination in protected soil — two life stages disguised by the same strategy. (Source: Current Biology, 2006)

☑ **Which Animals Voluntarily Amputate Their Own Body Parts to Survive?** Many lizard species shed their tails on demand through autotomy — breaking them at pre-built vertebral fracture planes. The detached tail thrashes independently for up to 20 minutes, distracting the predator. Starfish and crabs use equivalent mechanisms in their limbs. Lost parts typically regrow, though imperfectly, and the metabolic cost of replacement is significant. (Source: Herpetologica, 2004)

☑ **How Does a Sea Cucumber Turn Its Own Internal Organs Into a Weapon?** Sea cucumbers (Holothuroidea) respond to predator attack by contracting their body wall and expelling internal organs — stomach, intestines, respiratory trees — through a rupture point at the attacker. The ejected tissue may entangle or repel the predator. A complete set of replacement organs regenerates internally within three to six weeks. (Source: Invertebrate Biology, 2003)

☑ **What Defense Reflex Can Cause a Hagfish to Suffocate a Shark?** When bitten, the hagfish releases mucin protein from body pores that expands into a dense gel — hundreds of times its original volume — filling the predator's gills and interrupting breathing. Sharks that bite a hagfish typically release it immediately, not from pain but from suffocation. The slime dissolves harmlessly in open water within minutes. (Source: Integrative and Comparative Biology, 2010)

☑ How Does the Puffer Fish Make Itself Nearly Impossible to Swallow? When threatened, puffer fish rapidly ingest water to inflate an elastic stomach sac to three times their resting size within seconds. The resulting sphere has no graspable angle for a predator's jaws. Puffer fish are also toxic — a chemical backup ensuring that any predator persistent enough to swallow one rarely survives. (Source: Copeia, 2005)

☑ Can a Lizard Run Across Water to Escape a Predator? The common basilisk (Basiliscus basiliscus) escapes land predators by running across water on its hind legs. Lobed toes slap the surface fast enough to trap air pockets beneath each foot, generating upward force that prevents sinking. The technique works for up to 15 feet (4.6 m) before the lizard slows and switches to swimming. (Source: Nature, 1996)

☑ Why Does the Malaysian Exploding Termite Detonate Itself? The Malaysian exploding termite (Globitermes sulphureus) carries a large toxin gland nearly the length of its abdomen. Under threat, it contracts muscles until its body wall ruptures, spraying sticky, toxic fluid in all directions. The explosion kills the termite instantly but coats and immobilizes ant invaders — an irreversible colonial sacrifice. (Source: Journal of Chemical Ecology, 2012)

☑ **How Does a Cuttlefish Vanish in Under a Second?** The common cuttlefish (Sepia officinalis) executes up to 177 distinct camouflage pattern changes per minute — the fastest active concealment system in the animal kingdom. Unlike chameleons, which rely on slow hormonal pigment diffusion, the cuttlefish controls every chromatophore, iridophore, and papilla on its skin through direct neural commands from its brain, adjusting millions of skin units simultaneously. High-speed camera studies confirmed complete pattern transitions completing in under one second, allowing the animal to shift from a mottled rock texture to a sandy-bottom camouflage mid-pursuit, denying a predator any consistent visual target to lock onto. (Source: Journal of Experimental Biology, 1994)

☑ **Is the Opossum's Famous Death Act Actually a Choice?** When severely threatened, the Virginia opossum (Didelphis virginiana) collapses into a flaccid, unresponsive state that can persist for up to four hours. The animal is not faking consciously — it enters this state involuntarily via an extreme autonomic shock response, controlled by the nervous system rather than any deliberate decision. Heart rate drops, breathing slows to near-imperceptible levels, and the body releases a foul-smelling fluid from the anal glands. The opossum cannot snap out of it on command. Many predators instinctively avoid apparently dead prey, and the opossum has no control over when it wakes. (Source: Journal of Mammalogy, 1972)

☑ **Which Seabird Defends Its Nest by Projectile-Vomiting Onto Its Attacker?** The northern fulmar (Fulmarus glacialis) does not fight, flee, or inflate. When approached at its nest, it projects a stream of stomach oil up to five feet (1.5 m), produced by partially digested prey stored in a dedicated digestive chamber called the proventriculus. The oil coats feathers, destroying the waterproofing that seabirds depend on for thermal regulation. A falcon or great skua that receives a direct hit and cannot immediately clean its plumage may lose its ability to fly in cold conditions and eventually die of hypothermia. Fulmars have been documented repelling eagles, skuas, and human researchers with this response. (Source: Ibis, 1996)

☑ Why Doesn't the Anemone Ever Sting the Fish Living Among Its Tentacles? Sea anemone tentacles fire stinging nematocysts automatically when contact causes a chemical change at the cell surface. Clownfish (subfamily Amphiprioninae) are immune because their mucus coating lacks the surface chemistry that triggers the firing mechanism. Experiments removing the mucus layer and re-exposing fish to their host anemone produced immediate and severe stinging. The coating is not inherited — clownfish gradually acquire it by acclimating to an anemone with brief, increasing contacts over several hours. Fish reared in isolation have no immunity until they complete this conditioning process. The relationship is an earned truce, not a biological free pass. (Source: Journal of Experimental Marine Biology and Ecology, 1981)

☑ Do the Eyespots on a Butterfly's Wings Actually Mimic Owl Eyes? The conventional explanation — that butterfly wing eyespots mimic owl or hawk eyes and startle predators — turns out to be oversimplified. Research using artificial moths with modified eyespots showed that spots do not cause birds to flee as if confronting a larger predator. Instead, they redirect attacks toward wing edges. A bird targeting the eyespot strikes an expendable wing margin rather than the body. The butterfly loses a fragment of its wing but escapes with its body and flight muscles intact. Surviving butterflies in wild populations consistently show beak-mark damage around eyespots — direct field evidence of this deflection effect in action. (Source: Animal Behavior, 2005)

☑ **Why Is the Slow Loris the Only Primate With a Toxic Bite?** The slow loris (Nycticebus spp.) secretes a toxin from a gland on the inside of its elbow. By licking this gland and mixing the secretion with saliva, it loads a venomous compound directly into its mouth. A bite then delivers this into an attacker's wound. Slow lorises also rub the elbow-gland secretion onto their infants before leaving them in a tree during foraging — coating the vulnerable young in a chemical deterrent that renders them unpalatable to most predators. The defense is unique among primates: no other member of the order manufactures a toxin from an external body gland for delivery by mouth. (Source: Journal of Venomous Animals and Toxins, 2012)

☑ **How Does a Cobra Spit Venom Directly Into the Eyes of a Predator Two Body Lengths Away?** Mozambique spitting cobras (Naja mossambica) and their relatives project venom from forward-facing orifices in their fangs with enough force and accuracy to place droplets on a target's eyes from up to eight feet (2.4 m). Behavioral studies found that when a predator or human approaches, cobras track the movement of the face rather than the body, continuously redirecting the spit toward the eye region even as the target moves. Venom reaching the eye causes severe corneal damage and temporary or permanent blindness. The cobra needs no physical contact — incapacitation is delivered at a safe distance. (Source: Physiological and Biochemical Zoology, 2005)

☑ **Which Crab Builds Its Own Defense System From Living Organisms — and Transfers It When It Molts?** Decorator crabs (family Majidae) attach living sponges, anemones, algae, and bryozoans to their shells using specialized hooked hairs called setae. The chosen materials are not random: many species actively select the most noxious or stinging organisms available. Anemones placed on the shell sting predators attempting to bite; sponges contain distasteful chemicals; algae provide visual concealment. When a crab molts its old shell, it carefully removes each decoration and transplants it to the new exoskeleton before the new shell hardens. The camouflage is not passive — it is curated, maintained, and deliberately carried across life stages. (Source: Journal of Experimental Marine Biology and Ecology, 2001)

☑ **Which Crab Carries Live Stinging Weapons in Both Claws — and Clones Them When One Goes Missing?** The boxer crab (Lybia tessellata) of the Indo-Pacific holds a living anemone in each claw, brandishing them toward any approaching threat in a waving motion that brings stinging tentacles into direct contact with the attacker. This behavior is obligate — if a crab loses one anemone, it tears the remaining one in half. It allows both halves to regenerate into full anemones, a process researchers confirmed experimentally. Neither animal is harmed. The anemone receives transport across new feeding territory; the crab receives mobile living weapons that require no manufacturing, no replenishment, and no maintenance. (Source: Journal of Crustacean Biology, 2017)

☑ **Why Is a Skunk's Chemical Spray One of the Most Precisely Engineered Defense Weapons in the Animal Kingdom?** The striped skunk (Mephitis mephitis) produces thiol-based compounds detectable by humans at concentrations of one part per billion. The spray can be aimed with precision at a target's face from up to 10 feet (3 m), reaching peak accuracy at seven feet (2.1 m). Thiols bond to proteins in mucous membranes, causing immediate eye inflammation and temporary blindness. The only effective neutralizer is an oxidizing solution — hydrogen peroxide with sodium bicarbonate — that breaks sulfur bonds chemically. Washing with water spreads the compound rather than removing it, making the defense as chemically durable as it is initially potent. (Source: Journal of Chemical Ecology, 1990)

☑ **How Does a Fish School Explode Outward the Instant a Predator Strikes?** When a predator strikes the center of a schooling fish group, surrounding fish perform what researchers call the flash expansion: every individual accelerates radially outward simultaneously, bursting the school into fragments in a fraction of a second. The trigger is the lateral line detecting the pressure wave of the strike rather than visual cues — meaning the response propagates across the school faster than sight alone could carry it. High-speed cameras documented flash expansions covering 30 feet (9 m) in under 40 milliseconds. Each fish moves independently, but the synchronized outward explosion temporarily overwhelms a predator's ability to isolate any single target. (Source: Behavioral Ecology, 2000)

☑ **How Do Meerkats Protect Their Colony Without Stopping Its Foragers From Working?** Meerkat (Suricata suricatta) colonies post rotating sentinels at elevated positions while other members forage. The sentinel produces continuous "watchman's song" chirps confirming all is clear, and produces structurally distinct alarm calls for aerial versus terrestrial threats. Urgency is encoded in call rate — foragers run for burrows at the most urgent calls and merely pause for low-urgency ones, responding proportionately without interrupting productive foraging unnecessarily. When a predator approaches a juvenile, adults mob it collectively, surrounding it with aggressive posturing from multiple directions simultaneously — a cooperative response documented even from individuals with no direct genetic relationship to the threatened young. (Source: Behavioral Ecology, 2001)

☑ **Can a Sleeping Frog Become Nearly Transparent?** Glass frogs (family Centrolenidae) of Central and South America have translucent skin and muscle on their underside, making organs visible through the body wall. A 2022 study revealed they dramatically increase transparency during sleep by temporarily sequestering nearly 90% of their red blood cells into the liver, reducing light-absorbing hemoglobin in circulating blood by an equivalent amount. Sleeping glass frogs measured 34 to 61 percent more transparent than when awake. The mechanism — reversible red-blood-cell sequestration without causing clotting — is unique among vertebrates and has attracted attention from researchers studying human circulation management. (Source: Science, 2022)

☑ Which Ant Turns Its Own Body Into a Suicide Bomb to Defend Its Colony? Workers of Camponotus saundersi from Southeast Asia possess two oversized glands running nearly the full length of the abdomen, filled with a toxic, sticky secretion. When the ant contracts its abdominal muscles with sufficient force, the gland wall ruptures and the secretion is sprayed in all directions, coating and immobilizing attacking ants — often multiple enemies simultaneously. The explosion kills the defending ant instantly. Scientists confirmed that workers perform this autothysis voluntarily, and preferentially in defense of the colony rather than in direct response to personal threat — a form of calculated self-sacrifice calibrated to maximize collective benefit rather than individual survival. (Source: Naturwissenschaften, 1988)

☑ Why Can Only One of the 21 Living Armadillo Species Actually Roll Into a Ball? Of the 21 living armadillo species, only the three-banded armadillo (Tolypeutes tricinctus) of South America can roll into a complete, sealed sphere. Its back and head plates are proportioned and articulated differently from other species, allowing shell edges to meet and interlock when curled. The resulting ball has no gap a predator can pry open. Other armadillo species flee or press flat against the ground — their plates are protective from above. Still, they cannot form a closed enclosure because the underlying anatomy does not permit the required curl. The three-banded armadillo's complete rolling defense is the exception, not the rule, in its entire family. (Source: Journal of Morphology, 1979)

☑ How Does a Monkey Use a Single Sound to Govern 3 Miles of Rainforest? The mantled howler monkey (Alouatta palliata) generates its territorial roar through an enlarged, hollow hyoid bone at the throat base that amplifies calls like a resonating chamber. The call carries 3 miles (5 km) through dense rainforest canopy, advertising territorial occupancy without requiring any physical confrontation. Males roaring at dawn broadcast an audible map of their presence, reducing costly encounters with neighboring groups. A 2015 study found that males with a larger hyoid — a bigger vocal amplifier — had proportionally smaller testes: they invest in acoustic advertising rather than sperm competition, with one reproductive strategy physiologically precluding the other. (Source: Current Biology, 2015)

☑ How Does a Harmless Butterfly Survive by Pretending to Be Toxic? Batesian mimicry occurs when a palatable species evolves to resemble a toxic model, gaining protection without the metabolic cost of manufacturing toxins itself. The viceroy butterfly (Limenitis archippus) of North America closely resembles the monarch, which is unpalatable to most bird predators. A bird that has experienced a monarch avoids both species based on shared wing patterns. The mimicry only works when mimics remain rarer than their toxic model — if viceroys outnumber monarchs, predators encounter enough palatable individuals to risk sampling them, and the protective illusion collapses. The population ratio between mimic and model is the system's critical variable. (Source: Proceedings of the Royal Society B, 1991)

☑ Which Bird Swaps Its Entire Camouflage Wardrobe Twice a Year — and Times the Change Before the Landscape Shifts? The rock ptarmigan (Lagopus muta) undergoes three complete molts annually, producing distinct plumages for summer, autumn, and winter. The winter coat is entirely white — cryptic against snow — while the summer pattern of brown and black matches tundra rock and vegetation precisely. The timing is controlled by day length rather than temperature, ensuring the transition completes before the landscape changes rather than after. Males retain speckled intermediate plumage slightly longer each spring, as their snow-white coloration against bare tundra temporarily becomes a liability during courtship that must be balanced against the camouflage benefit it provides throughout the rest of the year. (Source: The Auk, 1993)

☑ Is Squid Ink Simply a Smokescreen — or Is It Chemically Attacking the Predator's Senses? When threatened, squid and cuttlefish expel ink from a dedicated gland mixed with mucus, forming a dense blob that holds its shape in water. Early researchers assumed this served purely as a visual screen. Later analysis revealed the ink contains tyrosinase, an enzyme that overstimulates a predator's chemosensory system, effectively jamming a shark's or moray eel's chemical senses rather than simply blocking vision. The blob also contains dopamine, which may further disrupt sensory function. Its three-dimensional persistence in water creates a body-sized decoy, drawing the predator's strike to an empty target while the squid retreats. (Source: Marine Biology, 1997)

☑ Why Can a Honey Badger Survive Snake Bites That Kill Animals Many Times Its Size? The honey badger (Mellivora capensis) has skin up to six millimeters (0.24 in) thick on its neck and back — tough enough that porcupine quills and many snake fangs cannot penetrate it. The skin is also loose-fitting, allowing the animal to twist inside its own hide to bite a predator holding it from behind. Honey badgers have survived documented direct bites from Cape cobras, puff adders, and black mambas, recovering from venom doses that kill domestic dogs many times their body weight. Research identified a molecular difference in their muscle acetylcholine receptors that reduces venom binding significantly compared to other mammals. (Source: PLOS ONE, 2012)

The Great Journeys

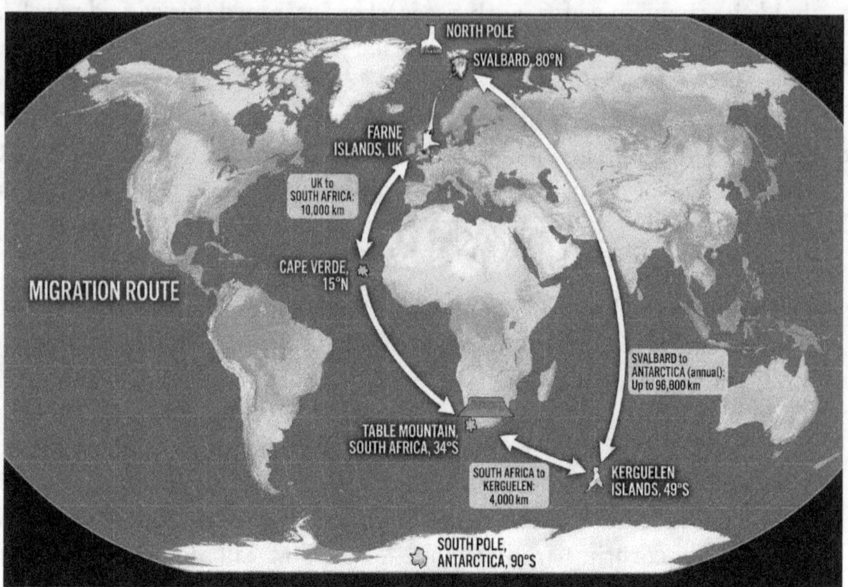

☑ **Which Bird Makes the Longest Migration of Any Animal on Earth?** The arctic tern completes an annual round trip of 44,000 miles (70,800 km) between its Arctic breeding grounds and Antarctic feeding waters — experiencing two polar summers in a single year. In 2010, researchers fitted 11 terns in Greenland and Iceland with miniature geolocators, tracking their complete routes for the first time. Rather than flying directly south, the birds followed S-shaped courses through the Atlantic, exploiting prevailing wind systems. Some individuals traveled nearly 49,000 miles (78,900 km) by choosing longer, wind-assisted paths. Their routes are not straight lines but optimized flight plans shaped by millions of years of selection. (Source: PNAS, 2010)

☑ **How Far Does an Arctic Tern Travel Across Its Entire Lifetime?** An arctic tern that survives for 30 years — a typical lifespan — accumulates approximately 1.5 million miles (2.4 million km) in migration alone, equivalent to three round-trip trips to the Moon. The 2010 geolocator study confirmed that individual birds complete the full 44,000-mile (70,800 km) annual circuit, while banding records show arctic terns regularly living 25 to 30 years in the wild. No other animal on Earth travels as far under its own power across a single lifetime. Every breeding season, they begin the circuit again from the opposite end of the world. (Source: PNAS, 2010)

☑ **How Does a Butterfly That Lives Only Six Weeks Complete a 3,000-Mile Migration?** No individual monarch butterfly (Danaus plexippus) completes the full 3,000-mile (4,800 km) round trip between Mexico and northern North America. A special long-lived generation undertakes the autumn migration — called the Methuselah generation — that survives up to eight months rather than the typical six weeks. This generation reaches the Mexican overwintering forests, survives winter, and begins flying north in spring, but dies before the return journey is complete. Three to five subsequent generations finish the northward leg in relay. The last autumn migrants are the great-great-grandchildren of individuals who never saw their winter home. (Source: USGS Monarch Monitoring Project)

☑ **Why Does a Pacific Salmon Stop Eating the Moment It Enters a River?** Chinook and sockeye salmon return from the Pacific Ocean and fight upstream to their natal tributaries — traveling up to 900 miles (1,450 km) against the current, scaling waterfalls and crossing shallows on stored energy alone. They stop feeding entirely at the river mouth, running on body fat and muscle as their jaws hook, their skin darkens, and their bodies physically deteriorate. After spawning, they die. Their decomposing carcasses feed eagles, bears, and wolves — but also fertilize streamside forests with marine-derived nitrogen, producing tree growth densities found nowhere else in the watershed. (Source: NOAA Fisheries)

☑ What Happens When 120 Million Crabs March to the Sea at Once? Every October or November, roughly 120 million Christmas Island red crabs (Gecarcoidea natalis) emerge from the island's forested interior and begin walking to the coast. The Australian government closes roads and builds dedicated crab-crossing bridges for the event, which cannot be diverted. Females release up to 100,000 eggs each into the sea, timing the moment to coincide with the last lunar quarter's high tide with extraordinary precision. Millions of crabs arrive at the cliff edge within days of each other after overland journeys of up to five days on foot across terrain that ignores no obstacle. (Source: Journal of Crustacean Biology, 2001)

☑ Which Bird Has Flown 7,500 Miles Without Landing, Eating, or Drinking? In September 2007, a bar-tailed godwit (Limosa lapponica) fitted with a satellite transmitter flew 7,500 miles (12,070 km) from western Alaska to New Zealand without once landing, eating, drinking, or sleeping — nine continuous days of flight. This remains the longest non-stop flight ever recorded for any animal. Before departure, the bird spent weeks nearly doubling its body weight in fat. During the crossing, its digestive organs shrank by 25%, freeing mass for additional fuel storage. It arrived weighing roughly half what it had weighed at takeoff, having converted its own internal organs into aviation fuel consumed entirely in transit. (Source: PNAS, 2008)

☑ How Does the Longest Mammal Migration Begin? Humpback whales (Megaptera novaeangliae) travel up to 10,000 miles (16,000 km) between polar feeding grounds in summer and tropical breeding waters in winter — the longest confirmed migration of any mammal. They eat almost nothing at the tropical end, sustaining months of life, singing, and nursing on fat reserves built during polar summers. A lactating female loses up to 25% of her body mass during this period. Crucially, the routes are culturally transmitted: calves learn specific ocean highways from their mothers, and different populations maintain distinct traditional pathways through water that carries no visible landmark of any kind. (Source: Animal Behavior)

☑ How Does a Bird Learn to Navigate by Stars Before It Has Ever Migrated? Young indigo buntings (Passerina cyanea) learn to navigate by identifying the center of the night sky's rotation — the fixed pivot point around which all visible stars appear to turn. This celestial anchor becomes their permanent navigational reference. Researcher Stephen Emlen demonstrated this by raising buntings under planetarium skies with rotation centered on a different star: every bird subsequently oriented toward the artificial pole rather than true north. The star compass is imprinted during a narrow developmental window in the first weeks of life, then retained and used accurately across years of subsequent migration. (Source: Science, 1969)

☑ What Guides a Leatherback Sea Turtle Across 10,000 Miles of Open Ocean? The leatherback sea turtle (Dermochelys coriacea) travels up to 10,000 miles (16,000 km) between nesting beaches and feeding grounds, crossing ocean basins without visible landmarks. NOAA satellite tracking confirmed leatherbacks navigate using Earth's magnetic field as a positional grid, detecting both magnetic inclination angle and intensity to establish geographic coordinates in open water. Course corrections documented during tracking showed individuals adjusting heading across thousands of miles with precision that researchers describe as extraordinary for a biological system using no manufactured instruments. Some individuals cross between the Atlantic and Pacific coasts of North America in a single annual cycle. (Source: NOAA Sea Turtle Program)

☑ Why Has No Scientist Ever Witnessed a European Eel Spawning? European eels (Anguilla anguilla) begin life as transparent, leaf-shaped larvae called leptocephali, drifting on Atlantic currents from their spawning ground in the Sargasso Sea. The journey to European rivers takes one to three years, carried entirely by the Gulf Stream without directed swimming. Once in freshwater, eels may live for 20 years before their bodies transform again for the return crossing of 3,100 to 4,700 miles (5,000 to 7,500 km) back to the Sargasso Sea, where they spawn and die. Despite this well-documented life cycle, no researcher has ever directly observed a European eel spawning event in the wild. (Source: Journal of the Marine Biological Association of the United Kingdom, 2008)

☑ What Transforms a Harmless Solitary Locust Into Part of a Biblical Plague? A desert locust (Schistocerca gregaria) living alone is a mild-mannered insect that avoids others and poses no agricultural threat. Crowding changes everything. When locusts make physical contact, repeated stimulation of sensory hairs on their hind legs triggers a serotonin surge within hours, permanently switching behavior: they become attracted to others rather than repelled, shift from solitary movement to marching, and begin forming swarms. Once this phase change cascades through a population, swarms covering 800 square miles (2,070 sq km) or more can form within days. The trigger is serotonin. The result is one of nature's most destructive forces. (Source: Science, 2009)

☑ How Do 1.5 Million Animals Decide Where to Cross a River? Each year, 1.5 million wildebeest (Connochaetes taurinus) circle a 500-mile (800 km) circuit through Tanzania and Kenya in pursuit of rainfall and fresh grass. The Mara River crossing is migration's most lethal moment: herds accumulate at the bank for days as individuals assess current speed and the crocodiles visible beneath the surface. When one animal commits, thousands follow within minutes. The crossing site is not random — herds consistently use locations where bank angle and water depth minimize losses. Researchers documented the same sites used repeatedly, suggesting accumulated knowledge shapes the decision rather than panic or chance. (Source: African Wildlife Foundation, 2015)

☑ **Which Annual Gathering Represents One of the Largest Concentrations of Mammals on Earth?** Every October and November, up to 10 million straw-coloured fruit bats (Eidolon helvum) converge on a two-square-mile (5.2 sq km) patch of swamp forest in Kasanka National Park, Zambia — one of the largest concentrations of any mammal species ever documented. The colony consumes an estimated 6,000 tons of fruit over eight weeks before dispersing across sub-Saharan Africa in every direction. Unlike most mass movements, the Kasanka gathering draws bats arriving from multiple directions rather than along a single corridor, making it a convergence rather than a migration endpoint. It remained unknown to science until the 1990s. (Source: Zoological Society of London, 2016)

☑ **How Does a Pacific Salmon Locate Its River Mouth After Years in the Open Ocean?** A 2013 University of North Carolina study demonstrated that sockeye salmon (Oncorhynchus nerka) use Earth's magnetic field not as a compass but as a GPS-like positioning system. By simultaneously detecting magnetic inclination angle and field intensity — two parameters that together define a unique geographic coordinate — salmon can triangulate their location anywhere in the North Pacific. Researchers replicated historical magnetic conditions from specific positions and found salmon reorienting to match real-world locations. The system is accurate enough to guide fish from mid-Pacific back to their natal river mouth across thousands of miles of featureless water. (Source: Current Biology, 2013)

☑ **What Allows a Bird Weighing Less Than a Nickel to Cross the Gulf of Mexico?** Every autumn, ruby-throated hummingbirds (Archilochus colubris) cross the Gulf of Mexico non-stop — approximately 500 miles (800 km) of open water for a bird weighing less than 0.2 oz (5.6 g), unable to land on water. Pre-migration hyperphagia allows some individuals to nearly double their body weight before departure, storing fat reserves consumed entirely during the crossing. A favorable tailwind makes the journey feasible; a headwind can render it physiologically impossible. Birds delayed by adverse weather mass on the Louisiana and Texas coastal vegetation, waiting for conditions to improve before committing to open water. (Source: The Condor, 1983)

☑ **Which Whale Migrates the Length of North America's Entire Pacific Coast?** The gray whale (Eschrichtius robustus) makes an annual round trip of approximately 10,000 to 14,000 miles (16,100 to 22,500 km) between Arctic feeding grounds in the Bering Sea and shallow breeding lagoons along the coast of Baja California, Mexico — one of the longest mammal migrations on Earth. Mothers with calves travel the coastline slowly, teaching the route to their young. After near-extinction from commercial whaling, the eastern Pacific population recovered to approximately 20,000 animals. Unlike oceanic migrants, gray whales travel in water often shallow enough for whale-watching vessels to sail alongside them at close range throughout the journey. (Source: NOAA Fisheries)

☑ **How Does a Female Sea Turtle Find Her Exact Hatching Beach After 20 Years at Sea?** Female loggerhead sea turtles (Caretta caretta) spend 20 to 30 years at sea before returning to reproduce on the beach where they hatched. Research confirmed they carry a magnetic map of their birth site encoded in infancy, defined by the combination of magnetic inclination and intensity at that coastal location. Decades later, this stored signature guides them back to within a few miles of their exact hatching site. Where magnetic field conditions have shifted over decades, nesting clusters have followed accordingly, confirming that the magnetic map, rather than scent or vision, drives the return. (Source: Current Biology, 2004)

☑ What Do Continental Radar Networks Reveal About Mass Bird Migration? Radar networks across the United States have revealed that migratory birds depart not gradually but in synchronized pulses driven by weather. The passage of an autumn cold front — tail winds, clearing skies — triggers departure decisions in billions of individual birds simultaneously. On peak migration nights, radar data have documented up to 400 million birds airborne over the eastern United States at once, all moving in the same direction without any leader or coordinating signal. Each bird makes an independent assessment; the apparent mass coordination is entirely emergent — billions of identical responses to the same meteorological cue. (Source: Science, 2018)

☑ How Far Does a Wandering Albatross Travel Without Flapping Its Wings? The wandering albatross (Diomedea exulans) does not follow a conventional migration route. Still, satellite tracking confirmed non-breeding individuals circumnavigating Antarctica continuously for months, covering hundreds of miles per day, almost entirely through dynamic soaring — extracting kinetic energy from wind gradients above ocean swells without sustained wing-flapping. Heart rate monitors showed some birds maintaining this travel with cardiac rates too low for powered flight, confirming motorless locomotion across the open ocean. No other bird species spends as large a proportion of its life aloft over open water, using the Southern Ocean's perpetual winds as its primary fuel rather than food. (Source: Nature, 1990)

☑ **What Did Satellite Tags Reveal About the Hidden Migration of European Cuckoos?** From 2011, the British Trust for Ornithology began attaching miniature satellite tags to common cuckoos (Cuculus canorus) departing Britain. The resulting data exposed two distinct migration routes to sub-Saharan Africa — one through Iberia, another through Italy and the eastern Mediterranean. The Italian route proved measurably more perilous, with birds using it showing lower survival rates when crossing the Sahara. Researchers also identified critical stopover sites in the Congo Basin rainforest that birds cannot complete the migration without. This previously unknown dependency makes British cuckoo populations directly vulnerable to deforestation happening thousands of miles from their breeding grounds. (Source: Nature Communications, 2016)

☑ **How Did Scientists Prove That a Butterfly Crossed the Atlantic Ocean?** The painted lady (Vanessa cardui) — the world's most widely distributed butterfly — was confirmed to cross the Atlantic from West Africa to South America, a journey of over 4,200 miles (6,760 km). Researchers analyzed hydrogen isotope ratios in wings of individuals collected in French Guiana, finding signatures matching African rainfall patterns rather than South American ones. Pollen grains on the butterflies identified specific West African plant species. The crossing takes place passively on equatorial trade winds at altitude, explaining how populations on both sides of an ocean, the insect cannot swim, remain genetically connected across generations. (Source: Nature Communications, 2024)

☑ **Could a Living Whale Remember Migration Routes From Before Industrial Whaling Began?** Bowhead whales (Balaena mysticetus) are confirmed to live over 200 years, making some individuals alive today old enough to predate large-scale commercial whaling in Arctic waters. Their seasonal migrations between Arctic summer feeding areas and Bering Sea wintering grounds follow specific corridors documented across decades of satellite tracking. Route knowledge is transmitted to younger animals by longer-lived pod members, creating navigational traditions that may span multiple human generations of continuous use. No other marine mammal combines extreme longevity with documented cultural route transmission, making bowhead pods among the oldest continuously maintained navigational lineages in the animal kingdom. (Source: Science, 2007)

☑ **How Does a Monarch Butterfly Compensate for a Sun That Moves 15 Degrees Every Hour?** A sun compass that fails to correct for the sun's movement would steer a southwest-bound monarch butterfly southeast by afternoon. Research at the University of Massachusetts confirmed that the compensating mechanism is located in the antennae, not the brain. Removing antennae caused monarchs to fly in random directions regardless of sunlight. Transplanting functional antennae from a second monarch restored directional flight; non-functional painted antennae did not. The antennal circadian clock recalculates solar bearing continuously, allowing monarchs to maintain a consistent southwestern heading across thousands of miles, with no individual ever completing the full round trip. (Source: Science, 2009)

☑ **How Do Geese Ride a Wave of Fresh Grass Northward Across an Entire Continent?** Each spring, the flush of new vegetation moves northward at 30 to 100 miles (50 to 160 km) per week as temperatures rise with latitude. Barnacle geese and other waterfowl track this advancing green wave precisely, stopping at each new flush of growth before it matures and loses nutritional value, then resuming northward flight as the wave progresses ahead of them. Satellite-tagged barnacle geese in Norwegian studies showed individuals stopping for one to three days per site, consistently arriving when plant protein content was highest and departing before nutrient quality peaked and then declined. (Source: Science, 2018)

☑ **Which Insect Weighing Less Than a Grape Seed Crosses an Entire Ocean?** The globe skimmer dragonfly (Pantala flavescens) crosses the Indian Ocean between India and East Africa — a journey exceeding 4,000 miles (6,400 km) — without any landmass to land on. Weighing approximately 0.03 oz (0.9 g), it rises to altitudes where seasonal monsoon winds carry it passively westward. Entomologist Charles Anderson confirmed the crossing by correlating the dragonfly's appearance in the Maldives with specific wind-pattern windows, then tracking the same weather systems through to East Africa. The globe skimmer is the world's most widespread dragonfly and likely the most widely distributed insect on Earth. (Source: PLOS ONE, 2016)

☑ What allows a Bird to Maintain Powered Flight Through Air With Less Than 30% Oxygen? Bar-headed geese (Anser indicus) cross the Himalayas during their annual migration, reaching altitudes of 29,000 feet (8,840 m) where oxygen availability is less than 30% of sea-level concentration. Data loggers implanted in migrating birds revealed they do not glide at altitude to conserve oxygen but flap continuously, sustaining high cardiac output under extreme hypoxia. Their hemoglobin carries an amino acid substitution that increases oxygen affinity at altitude, producing measurably superior oxygen capture compared to lowland goose species. The combination of modified hemoglobin and enlarged lung surface area makes this the most oxygen-efficient bird known. (Source: Journal of Experimental Biology, 2011)

☑ How Do Millions of Fish Navigate Together When No Individual Knows the Route? Schooling fish achieve collective navigation without any leader using three local rules per individual: match the speed and direction of nearest neighbors, maintain proximity without collision, and avoid anything moving toward you. Each fish responds only to animals immediately around it. Computational models and field tracking confirmed that the result is coherent movement that follows migration corridors, corrects for current drift, and routes around obstacles. Groups navigate more accurately than any individual fish alone because averaging the responses of thousands of independent agents cancels directional errors that would accumulate in a single navigator crossing open water. (Source: Animal Behavior, 2010)

☑ **Why Does Light Pollution Kill Hundreds of Millions of Migratory Birds Each Year?** Most songbird species migrate at night, using the rotating star pattern and Earth's magnetic field for navigation while resting during daylight hours. Light pollution has introduced a lethal complication: artificial lighting disrupts magnetic compass orientation, draws migrants into cities, and causes birds to circle illuminated buildings until exhausted. Cornell Lab of Ornithology estimates annual US building collision deaths at between 100 million and one billion individuals, with lit structures responsible for the majority. Switching off lights in tall buildings during peak migration windows in spring and autumn demonstrably reduces mortality in cities that have implemented the practice. (Source: Cornell Lab of Ornithology, 2019)

☑ **How Quickly Can a Bird Species Evolve a Completely New Migration Direction?** European blackcap warblers (Sylvia atricapilla) traditionally migrated southwest from Central Europe to sub-Saharan Africa every winter. Beginning in the 1960s, a small subset began wintering in Britain instead, drawn by garden feeding stations and mild Atlantic winters. By the 1990s, this northwest-migrating population was genetically distinct from the southwestern majority, partly because birds returning from Britain arrived at breeding grounds weeks earlier in spring and mated preferentially with each other. A new heritable migration direction was established in under 40 years — among the fastest documented cases of heritable route change in any vertebrate. (Source: Proceedings of the Royal Society B, 1992)

☑ **Which Land Animal Completes the Longest Terrestrial Migration in North America?** The Porcupine caribou herd — approximately 218,000 animals — completes an annual round trip of 3,000 miles (4,800 km) between boreal winter ranges in Yukon and Alaska and summer calving grounds on the Arctic Coastal Plain, crossing three international boundaries. Cows lead the spring migration at a pace exceeding 50 miles (80 km) per day, driven by the need to reach calving grounds before insect populations explode across the tundra. No other terrestrial migration on the continent involves as many animals covering as great a distance, and the herd receives no unified international protection across its full route. (Source: USGS Alaska Science Center)

☑ **What Is the Largest Migration on Earth?** Every night in every ocean, billions of zooplankton, small fish, squid, and crustaceans rise from depths of 650 to 3,300 feet (200 to 1,000 m) to near-surface waters to feed under darkness, then descend at dawn to avoid visual predators. This diel vertical migration is the largest daily movement of biomass on Earth — estimated at one to two billion tons of organisms making the same journey across every ocean basin. It also powers the ocean's biological carbon pump: organisms feeding near the surface then respiring at depth transfer carbon from surface waters into the deep sea at a scale influencing global climate. (Source: Nature, 2018)

☑ **Do Animals Ever Genuinely Get Lost During Migration?** Navigation errors in migration are documented regularly and carry a formal name: vagrancy. Juveniles migrating for the first time show measurably higher error rates than adults, with some species recording vagrant rates exceeding 20% in their first season. Individual birds, insects, and sea turtles straying far outside their expected range are recorded annually, particularly after storms push migrants off course. Vagrancy is not trivial: vagrant individuals that survive in new territory occasionally establish populations there, as documented in range expansions across multiple bird families. The white-tailed eagle returned to breed in Britain after decades of individuals arriving as Scandinavian vagrants. (Source: Ibis, 2015)

☑ **Which Bird Crosses the Open Atlantic Ocean on Its Very First Migration Without Any Guidance?** The American golden plover (Pluvialis dominica) breeds on Arctic tundra and winters in South America. Adults travel over approximately 2,400 miles (3,860 km) of open Atlantic with no landmass to stop on. Juveniles making their first migration must complete this crossing alone on stored fat — a 60 to 90-hour ocean flight with no adult guidance, no previous experience, and no second chance if conditions fail. Adults return via a different overland route through Central America. The juvenile Atlantic crossing is one of the most demanding first migrations of any bird species. (Source: The Auk, 1988)

☑ **Why Must White Storks Detour Hundreds of Miles to Avoid Open Water?** White storks (Ciconia ciconia) migrate between European breeding grounds and sub-Saharan wintering areas but cannot cross the open sea. They depend on thermal updrafts for soaring flight, and thermals do not form over water. This forces them to land-bridge routes: the western population funnels through Gibraltar while the eastern population crosses via the Bosphorus and Sinai. The two populations are genetically distinct, separated by a flyway boundary in Central Europe. A stork inheriting the wrong route faces an uncrossable sea at the expected crossing point, making route inheritance a critical survival requirement with no recovery option. (Source: Journal of Avian Biology, 2001)

☑ **Which Migrating Animal Travels by Locking Onto the Animal Directly Ahead and Never Letting Go?** Caribbean spiny lobsters (Panulirus argus) migrate up to 30 miles (48 km) from shallow feeding reefs to deeper spawning grounds, forming single-file queues of up to 65 individuals, each with its antennae in contact with the animal ahead. The tactile chain is hydrodynamically functional: individuals within a queue experience reduced drag compared to lobsters traveling alone and achieve higher speed at lower energy expenditure. The formation assembles when a lobster density encounters the same directional cue and requires no designated leader — it is an emergent structure maintained through physical contact between each consecutive animal. (Source: Marine Biology, 2001)

☑ **Why Is America's Most Ancient Migration Route Being Throttled to a Quarter Mile Wide?** The Sublette pronghorn (Antilocapra americana) herd follows a migration route of approximately 150 miles (240 km) between summer and winter ranges in Wyoming along a corridor ecologists estimate predates the last ice age. Highway fences and private land barriers have narrowed the path to a quarter mile (400 m) at certain bottlenecks, causing fatal crowding in drought years. The route has been designated the "Path of the Pronghorn". It carries federal protection in some sections — one of the few places in North America where a specific migration corridor has received named legal status. (Source: BioScience, 2005)

☑ **Which Seabird Circumnavigates the Entire Pacific Ocean Every Year for Food?** Sooty shearwaters (Ardenna grisea) breed on islands around New Zealand and complete a figure-eight circuit of the Pacific annually, recorded in a 2006 geolocator study as covering up to 40,000 miles (64,000 km) — one of the longest migrations of any vertebrate. After breeding, they fly northeast to feeding grounds off Alaska and California, arc westward toward Japan, and return south — exploiting summer in both hemispheres by never experiencing winter. The same birds return to the same burrow on the same island each year, navigating the entire Pacific basin on prevailing wind systems rather than directional wing-powered flight. (Source: PNAS, 2006)

☑ **What Did Data Loggers Reveal About a Bird That Spends Ten Months Continuously Airborne?** Common swifts (Apus apus) were long suspected to remain aloft for extended periods. Still, the full scale was confirmed in 2016 when researchers at Lund University equipped swifts with miniature geolocators and accelerometers. The devices confirmed non-breeding birds remain airborne for up to ten months — sleeping, feeding, drinking, and mating on the wing, descending only to nest. During sleep, swifts spiral upward on thermals and glide in slow circles consistent with controlled rest aloft. The annual distance covered per bird in continuous flight exceeds the distance from Earth to the Moon. (Source: Current Biology, 2016)

☑ **How Does an Arctic Predator Respond When Its Entire Food Supply Collapses in One Season?** Snowy owls (Bubo scandiacus) do not follow a fixed annual migration schedule. Instead, they make irruptive movements driven by prey cycles: when Arctic lemming populations crash, the owls' food supply collapses. Rather than starving, owls move south in thousands, appearing at airports, beaches, and rooftops outside their normal winter range. During the 2013–2014 irruption — the largest in decades — individuals reached Florida, Bermuda, and Texas. Tracking data revealed southward-moving birds were not naive juveniles wandering but healthy adults making a calculated nutritional decision: the Arctic was temporarily uninhabitable, and they left. (Source: Ornithological Applications, 2019)

☑ **Why Can a Shorebird's Entire Population Depend on One Beach for Ten Days Each Spring?** Red knots (Calidris canutus rufa) migrate approximately 9,300 miles (15,000 km) from Tierra del Fuego to Arctic breeding grounds. The entire subspecies population stops in Delaware Bay, timed to coincide with horseshoe crab (Limulus polyphemus) spawning on its beaches. In ten to twelve days, knots must nearly double their body weight on horseshoe crab eggs before the supply is exhausted and migration resumes. Declining horseshoe crab populations from overharvesting caused red knot numbers to fall over 75% between 1985 and 2005, demonstrating how a single stopover can determine the fate of an entire migratory subspecies. (Source: Science, 2006)

Minds of the Animal Kingdom

☑ How Did a Crow at Oxford Overturn Assumptions About Bird Intelligence? In 2002, Betty, a New Caledonian crow, spontaneously bent a straight wire into a hook to retrieve food from a tube — a behavior never seen in her species before, performed without any training. New Caledonian crows naturally manufacture hooked tools from plant stems in the wild, but Betty's wire-bending required solving a genuinely novel problem with an unfamiliar material. Subsequent Cambridge research confirmed the species completes multi-step sequential tasks, using one tool to retrieve another that accesses food — a cognitive chain previously attributed only to great apes. (Source: Science, 2002)

☑ **How Do Killer Whales Transmit Specific Behaviors Across Generations Without Genetic Change?** Different orca populations maintain behavioral traditions unexplainable by genetics alone. Off the Pacific Northwest, resident Chinook salmon-eating communities and transient mammal-hunting communities share the same waters but differ completely in diet, social structure, and hunting technique. Calves spend years observing and imitating their mothers; specific prey preferences and feeding methods are documented within individual maternal lineages but absent in adjacent populations. These transmissible behavioral signatures qualify orca societies as among the most culturally complex non-human animal groups yet identified — one of the few non-human populations where cultural identity demonstrably shapes survival behavior. (Source: Behavioral and Brain Sciences, 2001)

☑ **What Does a Chimpanzee Staring at Its Own Reflection Actually Tell Us About Consciousness?** In 1970, psychologist Gordon Gallup Jr. anesthetized chimpanzees, marked their foreheads with odorless dye, then presented them with mirrors. Upon waking, chimps reached directly for the marks on their own faces — behavior interpretable only if they understood the reflection as a self-representation. This mark test confirmed chimpanzees possess self-awareness: the ability to distinguish "self" from "other." Chimpanzees and orangutans reliably pass; gorillas and most other mammals typically fail. Whether passing the test implies consciousness as humans experience it, or simply self-modeling as a functional cognitive operation, remains scientifically contested. (Source: Science, 1970)

☑ **Do Elephants Grieve — and What Do the Bones of the Dead Mean to a Living Herd?** African elephants return to the remains of deceased group members, touching bones and skulls with their trunk tips in prolonged stillness. Cynthia Moss at Amboseli found elephants consistently identified and lingered over bones from their own group rather than strangers' — behavior suggesting individual recognition of the dead. Elephants also pass the mirror test: in 2006, a female named Happy at the Bronx Zoo repeatedly touched a white mark painted above her own eye while viewing her reflection, placing elephants among the small group of species confirmed to recognize themselves. (Source: PNAS, 2006)

☑ **Which Bird With No Neocortex Passed a Self-Recognition Test That Most Mammals Fail?** In 2008, Helmut Prior at Ruhr University Bochum placed small stickers on the throats of Eurasian magpies (Pica pica), visible only when the bird looked in a mirror. Five of five birds tested scratched the mark away while viewing their reflection — behavior interpretable only as self-directed. Magpies have no neocortex, the brain region long assumed to underlie self-awareness in mammals, yet they passed the identical test that gorillas typically fail. The result suggests self-recognition can emerge through entirely different neural architecture, in a brain far smaller than previously thought necessary. (Source: PLOS ONE, 2008)

☑ **How Does an Animal With No Centralized Brain Solve Puzzles, Escape Tanks, and Plan?** Two-thirds of an octopus's neurons are distributed through its eight arms rather than its central brain, making each arm semi-autonomous. Despite this unusual architecture, octopuses escape sealed tanks, open screw-top jars from the inside, and solve sequential puzzle boxes in controlled experiments. Otto, a captive individual at Coburg Aquarium in Germany, was documented repeatedly short-circuiting the tank's overhead lighting by squirting jets of water at the bulb. Whether this reflects conscious planning or arm-level intelligence reaching the same behavioral output remains unresolved — but the results are indistinguishable from deliberate problem-solving. (Source: Journal of Comparative Psychology, 1994)

☑ **Could a Gorilla Express Grief, Humor, and Regret Through Sign Language?** Koko, a western lowland gorilla taught American Sign Language by psychologist Francine Patterson from 1972, acquired more than 1,000 signs. She used them to mourn her pet cats, ask spontaneous questions, and describe unfamiliar objects — signing "finger bracelet" for ring. Critics argued her responses reflected skilled imitation and handler cuing rather than genuine linguistic understanding. Supporters noted she combined signs in novel sequences that no trainer had modeled. Whether Koko was genuinely using language or producing a sophisticated approximation of it remains one of the most contested questions in animal cognition. (Source: American Scientist, 1978)

☑ **Why Would a Wild Crow Teach Its Chicks to Mob a Human Face It Has Never Seen?** Researcher John Marzluff at the University of Washington trapped wild crows while wearing a rubber caveman mask. The birds scolded and dive-bombed the mask for years afterward, recognizing the specific face regardless of who wore it. They taught offspring and neighboring birds to respond to it. 12 years after the original trapping, crows across Seattle still mobbed researchers wearing the mask — second and third-generation hostility toward a face most of them had never personally encountered, maintained entirely through social learning and cultural transmission. (Source: Animal Cognition, 2012)

☑ **Can an Insect With One Million Neurons Grasp the Concept of Zero?** In 2018, researchers at RMIT University in Melbourne trained honeybees to associate symbols with number values, then tested whether they could identify "less than one" — placing a blank stimulus below all counted quantities. The bees chose the blank option correctly, demonstrating they understood zero as a quantity smaller than any positive number. A related study confirmed bees could learn to add and subtract by color-coded rules. Their brains contain roughly one million neurons — fewer than 0.01% of the human count — yet they performed operations requiring abstract rules previously demonstrated only in vertebrates with far larger brains. (Source: Science, 2018)

☑ **How Did Ravens Outperform Chimpanzees and Four-Year-Old Children in a Test of Foresight?** In 2017, researchers at Lund University presented ravens with a puzzle box openable only with a specific tool. After the ravens solved it, the tool was removed. An hour later, birds chose between the tool and several immediately rewarding distractors. Most selected the tool, ignored the food, and used it correctly when the box returned — after a 17-hour delay in subsequent trials. Ravens outperformed both chimpanzees and four-year-old children on the identical task, challenging the assumption that deliberate planning requires the complexity of a primate brain. (Source: Science, 2017)

☑ **Which Bird Deliberately Moves Its Hidden Food Stash When It Realizes It Was Being Watched?** Nicola Clayton and Anthony Dickinson at Cambridge found that western scrub-jays remember not only where they cached food, but what they hid and roughly when — the first documented episodic-like memory in a non-human animal. More strikingly, a bird observed caching by a dominant individual later relocated those caches when alone. Birds that had never stolen from others did not. The behavior requires understanding that the watching bird knows where the food is hidden — modeling another individual's knowledge state, a cognitive capacity scientists had assumed confined to humans and great apes. (Source: Nature, 1998)

☑ **Can a Bonobo Understand a Spoken English Sentence Without Being Trained to Do So?** Kanzi, a bonobo raised at the Language Research Center in Georgia, learned to use a lexigram keyboard — a board of abstract symbols representing words — not by being taught, but by watching his mother's unsuccessful lessons as an infant. Researchers later confirmed he understood complex spoken English sentences, including novel instructions he had never heard before, at a level comparable to a two-and-a-half-year-old human child. Kanzi spontaneously combined lexigrams to express original concepts, producing sequences like "bad surprise" or "chase hide." His learning appeared to depend critically on the early social immersion period, not formal instruction. (Source: Language Research Center, Georgia State University, 1993)

☑ Can a Dolphin Instantly Recognize "More" Without Counting? Bottlenose dolphins demonstrate numerical competency across multiple experimental formats. In controlled trials, they reliably selected the larger of two quantities of objects, correctly generalizing the rule to novel quantities without additional training. They also show subitizing — the immediate, pre-counting recognition of small quantities up to around four — a rapid assessment that bypasses sequential counting entirely. Research at the University of Hawaii by Louis Herman confirmed dolphins understand numerical relationships in symbolic formats as well as direct visual ones. Their numerical cognition appears to operate through mechanisms similar to those documented in human infants long before formal arithmetic is learned. (Source: Animal Cognition, 2003)

☑ Can a Monkey Grasp the Abstract Concept of Numerical Order — Not Just Learn a Sequence? Elizabeth Brannon and Herbert Terrace at Columbia University trained rhesus macaques to select four stimuli in ascending numerical order on a touchscreen. When tested on nine entirely new numerals never seen during training, the monkeys applied the rule correctly to the novel symbols at matching accuracy. They had learned the abstract concept of ascending order — not a memorized list of responses. The finding demonstrated that non-human primates can hold and apply numerical ordering rules independent of specific learned content, a cognitive capacity previously assumed to require human-level mathematical understanding. (Source: Science, 1998)

☑ Does the World's Smallest-Brained Animal to Pass the Mirror Test Actually Know What It Sees? In 2019, biologist Masanori Kohda at Osaka City University marked cleaner wrasse (Labroides dimidiatus) with spots visible only in mirrors, then observed fish scraping the mark against surfaces while viewing their reflection. The cleaner wrasse brain contains roughly 1,000 neurons — the simplest nervous system ever associated with mirror self-recognition. Critics argue the fish may simply be reacting to an unfamiliar mark as a potential parasite rather than recognizing itself. Whether this constitutes genuine self-awareness or a parasite-removal reflex exploited by the experimental design remains actively contested in the scientific literature. (Source: PLOS Biology, 2019)

☑ How Did One Dolphin's Innovation Spread Down Three Maternal Generations in the Wild? In Shark Bay, Western Australia, a specific matriline of bottlenose dolphins carries sea sponges on their rostrums while foraging on the seafloor. The sponge protects their beak from rough substrate and disturbs buried fish into the open. The technique was traced back to a single ancestor — nicknamed Sponging Eve — and passes from mother to daughter through years of observation. Sons rarely adopt it despite exposure. This is one of the clearest documented cases of a tool-use innovation spreading by strict maternal cultural transmission in a wild, non-captive animal population rather than genetic inheritance. (Source: PNAS, 2005)

☑ **How Did Wild Chimpanzees Prove That Non-Human Animals Can Have Regional Cultural Traditions?** Comparing tool behaviors across multiple African chimpanzee communities, researchers found the same species uses different techniques for termite fishing, nut cracking, and ant dipping in different locations. Taï Forest chimps crack nuts with stone hammers; Gombe chimps do not, despite sharing access to the same nut species and raw materials. The differences follow community lines, are transmitted from mother to offspring over years of observation, and cannot be attributed to ecological necessity or genetics. Published in 1999, this constituted the first systematic evidence for multiple distinct cultural traditions in a non-human species. (Source: Nature, 1999)

☑ **Why can a Dog Follow a Human Pointing Gesture That Even a Chimpanzee Cannot?** Brian Hare at Duke University showed domestic dogs spontaneously use human pointing and gaze direction to locate hidden food — a social ability chimpanzees show only unreliably with unfamiliar humans. Wolf pups raised by humans do not acquire it at comparable levels, suggesting it results from domestication rather than mammalian intelligence or exposure alone. Dogs appear to have been selected across thousands of years for the specific ability to read human communicative intent — an evolutionary tailoring of intelligence to a relationship that transformed the social brain of a predator into the most human-readable mind on Earth. (Source: Science, 2002)

☑ **How Fast Can a Wild Bird Population Learn a New Skill Through Social Observation Alone?** In 2015, Lucy Aplin at Oxford released wild-caught great tits that had learned a two-step puzzle-box solution back into their natural populations. Within days, untrained birds solved the puzzle by watching trained individuals, and the technique spread across the entire local population rapidly. Control groups with no trained birds showed negligible spontaneous solving. The study matched the spread to local social network structure, demonstrating that novel technical behavior can transmit through a wild vertebrate population at speed, confirming cultural learning operates in small-brained animals living under entirely natural conditions. (Source: Nature, 2015)

☑ **How Does a Bird Hide 30,000 Meals Across 200 Square Miles and Find Them Again Nine Months Later?** Clark's nutcrackers (Nucifraga columbiana) cache whitebark pine seeds each autumn, burying caches of four to five seeds across territories spanning up to 200 square miles (518 sq km). Each bird stores approximately 30,000 seeds in thousands of separate locations before winter. They recover the majority nine months later, even under several feet of snow, relying not on smell but on spatial memory anchored to specific landmarks. Biologist Alan Kamil confirmed their hippocampus is proportionally enlarged compared to non-caching species, suggesting the brain physically adapts to sustain this extraordinary feat. (Source: Journal of Experimental Psychology: Animal Behavior Processes, 1985)

☑ **Why Would a Well-Fed Rat Work Persistently to Free a Stranger Trapped in a Container?** In 2011, Inbal Ben-Ami Bartal and colleagues at the University of Chicago placed one rat inside a sealed tube while a free cagemate roamed nearby. Without training or reward, the free rat repeatedly worked to open the tube and release the trapped individual, then often shared food afterward. When the tube contained a chocolate chip, rats frequently freed their companion before eating. The behavior disappeared when the tube was empty, confirming that rats responded to distress rather than the container alone. The study provided the first controlled experimental evidence of empathy-driven prosocial behavior in rodents. (Source: Science, 2011)

☑ How Did a Member of the Crow Family Solve an Ancient Fable's Logic Puzzle Without Being Shown How? Aesop described a crow dropping stones into a pitcher to raise water within reach 2,500 years ago. In 2009, Christopher Bird and Nathan Emery at Cambridge University gave rooks (Corvus frugilegus) a tube containing a floating worm out of reach. Without any trial-and-error experience, several rooks immediately selected appropriately sized stones, dropped the correct number, and retrieved the worm once the water rose. They chose large stones over small ones and ignored the task when the tube held sand rather than water — demonstrating fluid causal reasoning. (Source: Current Biology, 2009)

☑ Can Great Apes Understand That Another Individual Holds a False Belief About the World? Theory of mind — grasping that another individual's beliefs can differ from reality — was long considered uniquely human. In 2016, Christopher Krupenye, Fumihiro Kano, and colleagues at Kyoto University fitted great apes with eye-tracking devices. He showed them videos of a human in a gorilla suit hiding behind a haystack. When the gorilla moved unseen, and the actor later searched for it, apes consistently anticipated the actor would look in the original hiding spot — even though they knew it was gone. Chimpanzees, bonobos, and orangutans all anticipated the actor's mistaken expectation without language. (Source: Science, 2016)

☑ How Did One Young Monkey's Discovery Change the Behavior of an Entire Population Within a Generation? In 1953, a young Japanese macaque (Macaca fuscata) named Imo on Koshima Island began washing sweet potatoes in a stream to remove sand. Within a few years, her mother and playmates adopted the habit; by 1962, most of the troop washed potatoes routinely. Imo later invented a second innovation: separating wheat from sand by throwing it into water and skimming off the floating grain. Researcher Masao Kawai documented both as the earliest clear evidence of cultural invention spreading through social learning in a non-human primate population. (Source: Primates, 1965)

☑ **What Does Playing Tag Have to Do With Being Smart?** Among vertebrates, species that play most elaborately tend to score highest on cognitive flexibility tests. Young ravens engage in aerial games with no survival function — dropping objects and catching them mid-air, repeatedly. Young elephants experiment with mud, sticks, and each other for hours beyond any nutritional need. Juvenile octopuses, despite being solitary animals unlikely ever to encounter siblings, engage with objects in controlled experiments when all survival needs are met. Gordon Burghardt, who developed the formal criteria for animal play, found that it concentrates in species with large brains relative to body size and extended juvenile periods. (Source: Behavioral and Brain Sciences, 2001)

☑ **How Did a Lab Rat in 1971 Unlock a Nobel Prize — and Reveal That Brains Build Internal Maps of Space?** In 1971, John O'Keefe at University College London recorded individual neurons in a rat's hippocampus during free exploration. Certain neurons fired only when the animal occupied one specific location — always that spot, never others. O'Keefe called them "place cells." May-Britt and Edvard Moser later discovered grid cells, providing a coordinate framework. Together, the findings established that the mammalian brain constructs a continuous, updatable spatial map of the environment — a biological GPS independent of visual landmarks — and earned the 2014 Nobel Prize in Physiology or Medicine. (Source: Brain Research, 1971)

☑ **Which Three Unrelated Animals Independently Arrived at the Same Idea: Using a Rock as a Tool?** Egyptian vultures (Neophron percnopterus) carry stones in their beaks and hurl them at ostrich eggs to crack the shell — one of the earliest documented examples of tool use in birds, observed across multiple African populations without social transmission. Sea otters float on their backs, balance a stone on their chest, and smash shellfish against it. Tuskfish (Choerodon fasciatus) on the Great Barrier Reef carry clams to coral heads and crack them open with precise strikes. Three lineages separated by hundreds of millions of years converged on identical mechanics. (Source: Nature, 1966)

☑ How Did a Cockatoo Invent a Tool It Had Never Seen in Its Life — Without Any Human Guidance? In 2012, Alice Auersperg and colleagues at the University of Vienna observed a Goffin's cockatoo (Cacatua goffiniana) named Figaro spontaneously tear a splinter from his wooden perch and use it to rake a nut fallen beyond reach. He was not trained; no demonstrator modeled the behavior. When the nut was replaced, Figaro made a new tool rather than retrieving the old one, selecting suitable pieces and rejecting others. This was the first confirmed case of spontaneous tool crafting in the parrot family — previously unknown to manufacture tools in the wild. (Source: Current Biology, 2012)

☑ Which Animals Can Silently Assess Rival Numbers Before a Confrontation — and Which Fish Can Count Its Shoal? Female lions in the Serengeti assess numerical odds before confronting intruders. Karen McComb and colleagues played recordings of one, two, or three unfamiliar lions roaring from hidden speakers: residents advanced confidently when outnumbering the simulated rivals. Still, they held back when recordings suggested disadvantage, even when strangers were invisible. Separately, studies on mosquitofish (Gambusia holbrooki) showed fish reliably choosing the larger of two shoals, discriminating between groups of three versus four — numerical assessment at a scale previously attributed only to vertebrates with significantly larger brains. (Source: Animal Behavior, 1994)

☑ Do Bumblebees Watch Each Other to Decide Which Flowers Are Worth Visiting? In 2005, Ellouise Leadbeater and Lars Chittka at Queen Mary University of London showed that bumblebees (Bombus terrestris) actively observe foraging conspecifics and use that social information to alter their own flower preferences. Naïve bees showed a demonstrator visiting a particular flower color, subsequently chose that color over alternatives, even when the reward value was identical, overriding prior experience. The finding established that social learning shapes foraging decisions in insects widely assumed to operate on fixed, genetically encoded rules — with implications for how innovations spread through wild pollinator populations. (Source: Current Biology, 2005)

☑ Can a Baboon Tell a Real Word From a Nonsense String — and What Does That Reveal About Reading? In 2012, Jonathan Grainger and colleagues at CNRS in Aix-en-Marseille trained olive baboons (Papio anubis) to discriminate English four-letter words from non-words on a touchscreen. After training on 500 word-nonword pairs, baboons correctly classified 75% of 7,832 novel examples they had never seen. They were not memorizing; they had internalized statistical regularities about which letter sequences look like words. The finding suggests the brain's capacity to detect visual statistical patterns — a foundation for reading — predates both language and the neural architecture previously considered uniquely human. (Source: Science, 2012)

☑ Why Do Animals That Live in Larger Groups Tend to Have Bigger Brains? Robin Dunbar at Oxford University analyzed neocortex-to-brain-volume ratios across 38 primate genera and found they correlated precisely with typical social group size. Species in larger, more complex groups had proportionally larger neocortices — the region responsible for higher-order cognition. Dunbar proposed that tracking relationships, alliances, deceptions, and hierarchies drove primate brain expansion over evolutionary time. His model predicted a maximum natural human social group of approximately 150 individuals — a figure matching independently measured clan sizes across diverse human societies worldwide. The hypothesis reframes intelligence as a social achievement, not a solitary one. (Source: Behavioral and Brain Sciences, 1998)

☑ **Can an Animal Know That It Doesn't Know the Answer — and Decide Not to Guess?** Metacognition — monitoring one's own knowledge states — was long considered uniquely human. In 1995, David Smith and colleagues at SUNY Buffalo gave rhesus macaques a memory test with a "decline to answer" option: subjects could skip a trial rather than guess. Macaques used the skip option disproportionately on trials they would have answered incorrectly and responded confidently on trials they would have gotten right. Monkeys that skipped difficult items outperformed peers forced to guess, providing the first rigorous evidence that a non-human primate can assess its own certainty before responding. (Source: Journal of Experimental Psychology: General, 1995)

☑ **Can a Horse Read a Human's Face — and Remember Whether That Person Looked Angry the Last Time They Met?** Horses distinguish between photographs of humans displaying positive versus negative expressions and retain that memory across separate encounters. Karen McComb and colleagues at the University of Sussex showed horses photographs of humans expressing anger or happiness, then introduced those people in person. Horses that had viewed an angry photograph exhibited markedly higher stress responses — faster heart rates and elevated muscle tension — even when the person arrived with a neutral expression. The study confirmed that horses store and apply emotional social memory across encounters with individual humans. (Source: Current Biology, 2018)

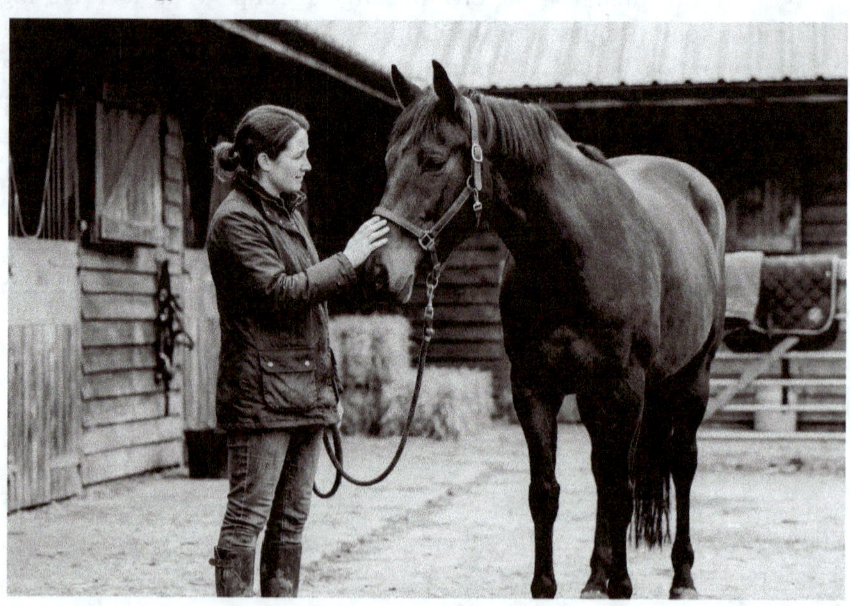

☑ How Long Have Wild Monkeys Been Cracking Open Food With Stone Tools in the Americas? In 2016, archaeologist Tomos Proffitt and colleagues excavating a cashew-processing site at Serra da Capivara in Brazil unearthed capuchin hammer stones and anvils dating back approximately 3,000 years. Wild bearded capuchins (Sapajus libidinosus) in the region still use nearly identical quartzite cobbles today, smashing cashew nuts on flat stone platforms in the same locations their ancestors used millennia ago. This constitutes the oldest archaeological evidence of tool use by any non-human primate outside Africa, demonstrating that systematic tool-use traditions in monkeys are neither recent nor learned from human contact. (Source: Nature, 2016)

☑ Why Would a Fish Follow a Route It Knows Is Inefficient Just Because the Rest of the Shoal Uses It? Guppies (Poecilia reticulata) trained to follow a roundabout route to food continued using it even when a shorter alternative was available — if they had learned the route by watching others. Kevin Laland and colleagues at St Andrews University showed that socially acquired preferences override individual efficiency: fish following the group stuck with the inferior path even after discovering the shortcut themselves. New fish introduced to the group learned the inefficient route from existing members. Social tradition in fish can thus be transmitted across individuals, perpetuating behaviors that offer no personal advantage. (Source: Behavioral Ecology, 1997)

☑ What Happened When Researchers Placed a Wooden Block Near Suspended Fruit and Watched an Asian Elephant Figure It Out? In 2011, Preston Foerder and colleagues at the City University of New York tested Asian elephants (Elephas maximus) with fruit suspended beyond reach. Elephants initially wandered away. After an interval, several returned, located a wooden block in the enclosure, pushed it beneath the fruit without prompting, stood on it, and retrieved the reward — a single purposeful sequence, not trial-and-error. The finding placed elephants among the rare species confirmed to solve novel spatial problems through insight: the sudden reorganization of a problem rather than incremental learning. (Source: PLoS ONE, 2011)

A Note From The Author

———————— ◆ ————————

Enjoying the Facts So Far?

If a fact surprised you, made you look something up, or sparked a conversation — that's exactly what this series is for.

An honest review — even just a sentence — makes an enormous difference for an independent author. It helps other curious readers find books like this one, rather than settling for content that recycles unverified myths.

Leave Your Review Here

Scan to go directly to the series page. Your honest thoughts — good or mixed — help the right readers find this book.

———————— ◆ ————————

TRUE VERIFIED FACTS • FUN & INTRIGUING FACTS
BOOKS SERIES

Extreme Lives

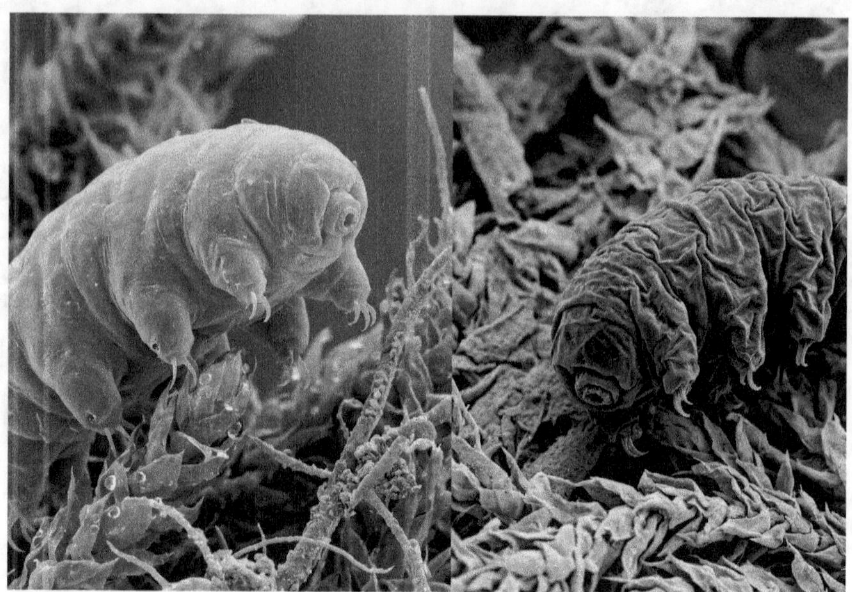

☑ What Animal Can Survive Conditions That Would Kill Every Other Known Species? The tardigrade — a microscopic eight-legged invertebrate less than 0.02 inches (0.5 mm) long — enters a suspended state called cryptobiosis when conditions become lethal. It expels 97% of its body water, pulls its legs inward, and shrivels into a desiccated structure called a "tun." In this state, metabolism drops to a fraction of a percent of normal. The animal no longer eats, breathes, or reproduces, yet it remains biologically viable. When moisture returns, even after decades of waiting, the tun rehydrates, and the tardigrade walks away intact. (Source: International Journal of Astrobiology, 2012)

☑ How Extreme Can Tardigrade Survival Get? In cryptobiosis, tardigrades survive radiation doses more than 1,000 times lethal to humans, pressures six times greater than those found in the deepest ocean trench, and the hard vacuum of open space. Researchers at the European Space Agency exposed tardigrades in their tun state to direct, unfiltered solar radiation in low Earth orbit for ten days. The majority survived and revived normally on return. No other animal achieves anything close to this combination of tolerances, which is why astrobiologists treat tardigrades as a template for theorizing what life on other worlds might endure. (Source: Current Biology, 2008)

☑ How Does a Frog Survive Being Frozen Solid for Months? Each autumn, the wood frog (Rana sylvatica) of North America freezes solid. Its heart stops, breathing ceases, and up to 65% of its body water turns to ice. No antifreeze protein prevents freezing — the frog freezes completely. What prevents death is glucose: the liver floods the bloodstream with sugar before freezing begins, which draws water out of cells and replaces it with a cryoprotective syrup. In spring, the frog thaws within hours, its heart restarts, and it hops away with no lasting tissue damage. (Source: Journal of Experimental Biology, 1992)

☑ Which Animal Lives Where the Water Temperature Would Cook Most Fish Alive? The Pompeii worm (Alvinella pompejana), discovered at hydrothermal vent fields on the East Pacific Rise, builds papery tubes directly on vent chimneys where water temperature reaches 176 degrees F (80 degrees C). While its tail end sits in this near-boiling flow, its head extends into cooler surrounding water around 72 degrees F (22 degrees C). The worm hosts heat-tolerant bacteria in a thick fleece across its back that appear to help buffer the extreme temperature gradient. It remains the most heat-tolerant complex animal science has confirmed. (Source: Science, 1998)

☑ How Old Is the Oldest Living Vertebrate on Earth? The Greenland shark (Somniosus microcephalus) grows at roughly half an inch (1 cm) per year — one of the slowest growth rates of any vertebrate. A 2016 study used radiocarbon dating of proteins in the eye lens, which form before birth and accumulate no new material afterward, to estimate the age of 28 specimens. The largest, a female measuring 16.5 feet (5 m), was calculated to be at least 392 years old, with a probable age of 512 years. It was alive before Shakespeare wrote his plays. (Source: Science, 2016)

☑ What Does the Greenland Shark's Extraordinary Lifespan Mean for Its Biology? Because the Greenland shark grows so slowly, it does not reach sexual maturity until approximately 150 years of age — the longest juvenile period of any known vertebrate. A shark reproducing for the first time today was born around 1875. It survives in the near-freezing waters of the Arctic and North Atlantic, barely moving, its lethargic pace essential to conserving energy in an environment that provides almost nothing to eat. Scientists believe extreme cold itself may be the primary driver of its astonishing longevity — a biological dividend of permanent near-zero temperatures. (Source: Science, 2016)

☑ How Do Animals Survive the Crushing Pressure of the Deep Ocean? At the bottom of the Mariana Trench, 36,089 feet (10,994 m) below the surface, water pressure reaches eight tons per square inch (1,100 bars) — more than 1,000 times the atmospheric pressure humans experience at sea level. Animals at these depths do not fight this force. Their cells contain water rather than gas, making them nearly incompressible. Proteins and cell membranes are stabilized by pressure-adapted molecules called piezolytes, which prevent compression from disrupting biochemistry. There are no air-filled cavities to collapse — a design so effective it sustains life at the deepest point on Earth. (Source: Annual Review of Marine Science, 2014)

☑ What Fish Lives Deeper Than Any Other — and How Does It Function Under That Pressure? The Mariana snailfish (Pseudoliparis swirei) was filmed at 26,831 feet (8,178 m) in 2017, and a related species was recorded at 27,349 feet (8,336 m) in 2023 — the deepest fish ever confirmed. Rather than solid bones, snailfish have a gelatinous, unfused skeleton that flexes under pressure rather than shattering. Their cells carry high concentrations of trimethylamine oxide, a pressure-counteracting molecule that keeps proteins functional at depths where most biological structures would cease working entirely. (Source: Nature Ecology & Evolution, 2023)

☑ Which Animals Have Taken Over Chernobyl's Radioactive Exclusion Zone? Forty years after the 1986 nuclear disaster, the Chernobyl Exclusion Zone has become an accidental wildlife sanctuary. With humans removed, gray wolves, lynx, Eurasian brown bears, Przewalski's wild horses, and hundreds of bird species have repopulated in numbers rarely seen in the surrounding occupied regions. Camera trap surveys found wolf densities seven times higher inside the zone than in comparable, uncontaminated protected areas nearby. The evidence from Chernobyl suggests that sustained human presence is more damaging to large wildlife populations than radiation exposure at moderate chronic doses. (Source: Current Biology, 2015)

☑ What Does Chernobyl Reveal About Radiation's Long-Term Effects on Smaller Animals? Despite the recovery of large mammals, studies of smaller organisms tell a different story. Barn swallows breeding near the most contaminated areas show higher rates of albinism, reduced brain volume, and lower reproductive success compared to those farther from the reactor. Rodents in heavily contaminated zones carry measurable chromosomal abnormalities. Soil invertebrates in the Red Forest — where trees turned orange and died in 1986 — remain significantly reduced in diversity. For large, mobile animals, the absence of humans outweighs the radiation burden. For small, stationary organisms, it does not. (Source: Biological Conservation, 2016)

☑ **How Does a Fish Survive for Years Without Water?** When African rivers dry up, the lungfish (Protopterus species) burrows into the mud, secretes a mucus cocoon around itself, and enters aestivation. This deep metabolic suspension can last up to five years. Its metabolic rate drops by 98%, organs slow to a near standstill, and it survives by breaking down its own muscle tissue for energy. When the rains return, and the mud softens, the lungfish rehydrates, breathes, and resumes normal life. Fossil records show that lungfish have used this same survival strategy for at least 400 million years without major modification. (Source: Journal of Experimental Biology, 2003)

☑ **Which Is the Only Vertebrate on Earth With No Red Blood Cells?** Antarctic icefish (family Channichthyidae) are the only vertebrates without hemoglobin. Their blood is colorless — a ghostly, milky white. They survive by absorbing oxygen directly through their scaleless skin and circulating vast volumes of blood using outsized hearts and unusually wide blood vessels. Their blood volume is approximately four times greater than that of comparable fish. This entire solution evolved because cold Antarctic waters hold far more dissolved oxygen than warm seas, making hemoglobin unnecessary — an extraordinary case of evolution discarding a molecule that every other vertebrate depends on completely. (Source: Journal of Experimental Biology, 2006)

☑ **How Do Animals Survive Months Without a Single Meal?** The champions of food restriction do not simply endure hunger — they physiologically restructure. Burmese pythons shrink their intestines, liver, and heart between meals, then regenerate these organs within days of consuming prey, cutting metabolic running costs dramatically while fasting. Large sharks enter sustained metabolic suppression for months between significant kills. Spiders have survived more than two years without food under laboratory conditions, their resting metabolism dropping to near-baseline. In each case, the body becomes an engine that throttles down to its minimum rather than one that simply runs empty and fails. (Source: Journal of Experimental Biology, 1998)

☑ How Does a Bear Spend Six Months Without Eating, Drinking, or Producing Waste? Black and grizzly bears enter dormancy — not true hibernation — in which body temperature drops only five to eight degrees F (three to five degrees C), yet metabolic rate falls by up to 75%. During this period, they do not urinate or defecate. Nitrogen waste from muscle breakdown is reprocessed back into protein rather than excreted — preventing the muscle loss that would normally follow months without food. Females give birth, nurse cubs, and emerge in spring with minimal wasting. Researchers are studying this nitrogen recycling as a potential treatment for human muscle-wasting diseases. (Source: Science, 2011)

☑ Which Mammal Has Never Been Observed Developing Cancer Under Laboratory Conditions? The naked mole rat (Heterocephalus glaber) appears to be cancer-immune. Scientists have maintained colonies for decades without a single confirmed case of spontaneous cancer. Their cells produce a high-molecular-weight form of hyaluronan — a tissue-stiffening sugar — that prevents cells from crowding together, halting cancerous proliferation before it can establish. They are also nearly insensitive to acid-induced pain due to an altered sodium channel that blocks the relevant pain signal. Both features are under active investigation for human medical applications, making the naked mole rat one of the most scientifically studied small mammals alive. (Source: Nature, 2013)

☑ Why Does the Naked Mole Rat Live Ten Times Longer Than Any Similar-Sized Rodent? A mouse of equivalent body size lives two to three years. The naked mole rat lives up to 37 years — the longest confirmed lifespan of any rodent. It shows almost no measurable decline in physiological function, cancer risk, or reproductive capacity with age, defying what biologists call Gompertz's Law — the mathematical rule describing how mortality risk doubles at regular intervals throughout a mammal's life. Unlike mice, naked mole rats show no increase in mortality rate after reaching adulthood, a pattern of biological aging never previously documented in any mammal and still not fully explained. (Source: eLife, 2018)

☑ How Can a Shrimp Be Bone-Dry for Decades and Still Come Back to Life? Brine shrimp (Artemia salina) produce dormant cysts that survive complete desiccation for years — even decades — then hatch the moment water reaches them. These cysts have been revived after 25 years of dry storage and after exposure to temperatures as low as -320 degrees F (-196 degrees C). Their survival mechanism relies on trehalose, a sugar that replaces cell water during desiccation, forming a glass-like matrix that preserves biological structures intact. This molecular mechanism is now actively used in pharmaceutical research to preserve vaccines and biological samples without refrigeration. (Source: Integrative and Comparative Biology, 2004)

☑ How Does the Snow Leopard Survive Year-Round at the World's Highest Elevations? The snow leopard (Panthera uncia) lives permanently at elevations of 10,000 to 18,000 feet (3,000 to 5,500 m) across Central Asia — higher than almost any other large predator on Earth. Its oversized nasal cavities warm and humidify thin, frigid air before it reaches the lungs. Chest and lung capacity are proportionally larger than those of lowland cats. Dense underfur insulates in temperatures dropping to -40 degrees F (-40 degrees C). Wide, fur-covered paws distribute weight across deep snow and grip bare rock simultaneously — a package of adaptations no single engineering design principle could improve upon. (Source: Panthera, 2020)

☑ Which Small Mammal Lives Higher Than Almost Any Other — and Dies if It Gets Too Warm? The American pika (Ochotona princeps) lives in rocky slopes above 11,000 feet (3,353 m), making it one of the highest-altitude small mammals in North America. It cannot thermoregulate effectively at temperatures above 78 degrees F (25.5 degrees C) and dies from overheating within hours of sustained warmth. This narrow thermal tolerance makes it one of the most climate-sensitive mammals on the continent. Pika populations have retreated upslope by an average of 900 feet (274 m) over the past century, and some lowland populations have disappeared entirely, with no cooler habitat remaining above them. (Source: Global Change Biology, 2003)

☑ Why Do Nine Out of Ten Deep-Sea Animals Produce Their Own Light? In the deep ocean below 3,300 feet (1,000 m), approximately 90% of species produce bioluminescence — a cold chemical light generated when the enzyme luciferase acts on a substrate called luciferin in the presence of oxygen. This light serves multiple functions across different species: attracting prey into the dark, signaling potential mates, blinding predators with sudden flashes, and providing counterillumination camouflage against faint light filtering from above. Bioluminescence has evolved at least 40 separate times independently in different animal lineages, making it one of the most frequently reinvented solutions in the entire history of evolution. (Source: MBARI, 2010)

☑ **Which Mammal Hibernates So Deeply That Its Blood Temperature Drops Below Freezing?** The Arctic ground squirrel (Urocitellus parryii) is the only warm-blooded animal whose core body temperature falls below 32 degrees F (0 degrees C) during hibernation — recorded as low as 26.6 degrees F (-3 degrees C), colder than the frozen ground in some dens. Its blood does not freeze because tissues actively suppress ice crystal nucleation through supercooling, a process not yet fully explained at the molecular level. Every two to three weeks, the body rewarms to near-normal temperature at extreme energy cost before cooling again — a cycle repeated up to 18 times across a seven-month hibernation. (Source: Journal of Experimental Biology, 2002)

☑ **How Does the World's Fastest Heartbeat Slow by 97% Every Single Night?** Hummingbirds beat their hearts up to 1,200 times per minute in flight and burn energy faster than almost any other vertebrate. To survive the night without food, many species enter torpor: body temperature falls from 104 degrees F (40 degrees C) to as low as 48 degrees F (9 degrees C), and heart rate drops below 50 beats per minute. A hummingbird in torpor is unresponsive to sound and touch. Morning arousal takes up to an hour and burns as much energy as several hours of normal sleep. Without this nightly shutdown, most species would starve before dawn. (Source: Physiological and Biochemical Zoology, 2001)

☑ **Which Animal Lives a Century in Total Darkness and survives for over a Decade Without Food?** The olm (Proteus anguinus), a blind cave salamander found in underground rivers of Slovenia and Croatia, lives to approximately 100 years — the longest confirmed lifespan of any salamander. It reaches sexual maturity only around age 16. During famines lasting more than 12 years, it reduces its metabolic rate to near-zero and reabsorbs its own tissue for energy. The entire pace of its life is calibrated for an environment where food is rare, light is absent, and movement is a waste of resources — a biology built for extreme patience rather than extreme speed. (Source: Biology Letters, 2010)

☑ **How Does an Animal Born Blind Navigate Pitch-Black Caves With No Landmarks at All?** The olm forms eyes normally in the embryo, but they degenerate beneath the skin after hatching — vestigial remnants sealed under tissue. Evolution compensated by amplifying every other sense. Specialized cells in the skin detect weak electric fields, allowing orientation within Earth's geomagnetic field across featureless cave passages. Chemoreceptors in the snout identify molecular traces dissolved in underground water with exceptional sensitivity. Pressure-sensing organs register the faintest movement nearby. In permanent darkness, the olm navigates with a sensory toolkit that, in its own domain, exceeds what most sighted animals achieve in full light. (Source: Journal of Zoology, 2009)

☑ **Which Ant Races Across Sand Hot Enough to Kill It in Under a Minute?** The Saharan silver ant (Cataglyphis bombycina) forages at midday when ground surface temperatures reach 140 degrees F (60 degrees C) — a thermal zone lethal to every other desert insect. Its safe forage window is roughly ten minutes. Triangular silver hairs reflect solar radiation from above and from the superheated ground, reducing body temperature by several degrees. Thermosensors in the feet detect the approach of the lethal threshold and trigger return to the nest. During those ten minutes, it moves at up to 108 body lengths per second — the fastest relative speed of any measured ant. (Source: PLOS ONE, 2015)

☑ **What Engineering Principle Allows a Desert Beetle to Harvest Drinking Water from Fog?** The Namib Desert fog-basking beetle (Stenocara gracilipes) survives in an environment where rain may not fall for years, extracting water from coastal fogs instead. It faces into the wind and tilts its back toward incoming mist. Raised bumps on its shell are coated in hydrophilic material that attracts water molecules; surrounding surfaces carry hydrophobic wax that repels them. Droplets accumulate on the bumps until they are heavy enough to roll down into the beetle's mouth. The design is so precisely effective that materials scientists have replicated its micro-architecture for water-harvesting surfaces deployed in arid regions worldwide. (Source: Nature, 2001)

☑ What Makes the Fennec Fox's Enormous Ears Its Primary Survival Tool in the Sahara? The fennec fox (Vulpes zerda) carries ears up to six inches (15 cm) long — proportionally the largest of any fox relative to body size. In the Sahara's 130-degree-F (54-degree-C) heat, these ears function primarily as heat radiators rather than sound collectors. A dense network of blood vessels runs close to the ear surface, venting heat by convective cooling as air flows across them. This lowers core body temperature without sweating — critical where water may be unavailable for weeks. The same ears also detect prey moving underground, making one structure serve two survival functions simultaneously. (Source: African Journal of Ecology, 2004)

☑ How Does a Polar Bear Keep Newborn Cubs Alive Without Eating for Five Months? A pregnant polar bear (Ursus maritimus) digs a den in October and does not emerge for up to five months without eating, drinking, or defecating. Inside, her body heat alone raises air temperature to near 32 degrees F (0 degrees C) even as external temperatures reach -40 degrees F (-40 degrees C). Cubs are born in December at just 1 lb (450 g) — among the smallest newborns of any placental mammal — and nurse exclusively from the mother's fat reserves, reaching 20 to 25 lb (9 to 11 kg) before the family emerges in spring. (Source: Journal of Mammalogy, 1990)

☑ **What Allows a Seal to Stay Submerged for Over an Hour With No External Oxygen Supply?** The Weddell seal (Leptonychotes weddellii) routinely dives for 45 to 80 minutes, reaching 1,969 feet (600 m) beneath sea ice. Rather than storing oxygen in its lungs, it carries oxygen in blood and muscles: blood volume is 50% greater than a human's, with hemoglobin concentrations three times higher. Muscle myoglobin stores additional oxygen, giving the flesh a dark, near-black color. As it descends, flexible ribs allow the lungs to collapse completely, preventing nitrogen from dissolving into the blood, causing decompression sickness. The seal uses a breathing hole kept open by gnawing at refreezing ice. (Source: Journal of Experimental Biology, 1985)

☑ **What Prevents Diving Mammals From Being Crushed by Water Pressure at Depth?** As marine mammals descend to extreme depths, pressure compresses the chest cavity. Dolphins, seals, and whales exhibit a blood-shift response: blood and fluid migrate from the periphery into the chest, filling spaces around compressing organs and equalizing internal and external pressure as the lungs collapse. Peripheral vessels constrict sharply, diverting circulation to the heart and brain. Muscles switch to anaerobic metabolism, and heart rate slows by up to 90%. This cascade of involuntary responses — coordinated without conscious control — prevents crushing injury and decompression sickness during dives that would be fatal to any terrestrial mammal within seconds. (Source: Proceedings of the Royal Society B, 2007)

☑ **Which Raptors Have Been Documented Deliberately Carrying Fire to Flush Out Prey?** Black kites, whistling kites, and brown falcons in northern Australia — collectively called fire-hawk raptors — have been documented picking up burning sticks from active wildfire fronts and dropping them in unburned grass ahead of the fire line to flush fleeing prey. Published accounts from 2018 include multiple independent witnesses describing birds carrying smoldering branches across firebreaks to extend burn zones. If confirmed as intentional, these raptors would be the only non-human animals documented to spread fire deliberately — a behavior Aboriginal communities in northern Australia have named and recognized for generations. (Source: Journal of Ethnobiology, 2018)

☑ **Which Beetle Detects a Wildfire from 50 Miles Away and Arrives Before the Flames Go Out?** The black fire beetle (Melanophila acuminata) detects infrared radiation from burning forests through pit organs on its thorax, sensing heat from up to 50 miles (80 km) away. It flies into the smoldering perimeter of active fires to lay eggs beneath charred bark, where larvae face zero competition and abundant food in dead wood. After fire passes, burned landscapes attract black-backed woodpeckers — which nest exclusively in recently charred forest — and release serotinous pine seeds sealed for decades by resin. For a guild of species, wildfire is not destruction but an ecological invitation. (Source: Journal of Chemical Ecology, 1994)

☑ **How Can a Seabird Survive Inside a Tropical Cyclone Without Landing for Days?** In 2016, researchers satellite-tracked great frigatebirds (Fregata minor) during a tropical cyclone over the Indian Ocean. Rather than fleeing, the birds soared within and around the eye, exploiting rising air inside the eyewall to remain aloft without flapping for hours. One individual rode storm thermals for more than a day. Frigatebirds cannot land on water — their plumage is not waterproof — so stopping was impossible. Their strategy was exploitation rather than escape: using the storm's aerodynamic structure as a free energy source to cross hundreds of miles of open ocean on the hurricane's own engine. (Source: Science, 2016)

☑ Which Shore Animal Survives Rock Temperatures Over 120 Degrees and Wave Forces in the Tons? Intertidal limpets (Patella species) cling to rock that heats to over 120 degrees F (49 degrees C) in summer sun, then are submerged in cold seawater twice daily. During air exposure, the limpet clamps its shell flat against the rock to minimize water loss and insulate soft tissue from peak surface heat. Its muscular foot generates suction of 70 lb per square inch (4.8 kg per square centimeter), withstanding breaking waves that deliver forces measured in tons. Between thermal and mechanical extremes that would destroy most organisms within minutes, limpets survive for 20 years or more. (Source: Journal of Experimental Biology, 2004)

☑ What Bonds Itself to Rock Using the Strongest Biological Adhesive Ever Measured? Barnacles produce a cement that cures underwater and achieves tensile strength exceeding 5,000 lb per square inch (350 bars) — the strongest biological adhesive documented, outperforming marine-grade epoxy in wet conditions. It works by displacing water molecules at the bonding surface before polymerizing into a cross-linked protein matrix. A fixed barnacle faces twice-daily air exposure, wave impact, salt encrustation, and temperature swings of 90 degrees F (50 degrees C) within each tidal cycle, yet the bond holds for years without renewal. Scientists are attempting to synthesize the compound for surgical tissue repair, where standard adhesives fail in blood. (Source: Langmuir, 2011)

☑ Are Thousands of Living Tardigrades Currently Sitting Intact on the Surface of the Moon? In April 2019, the Israeli lunar lander Beresheet crashed on the Moon, scattering its payload — which included thousands of tardigrades in dehydrated tun form stored on a synthetic DNA archive. Because the Moon has no weather, no liquid water, and no atmosphere to drive degradation, the tardigrades remain physically intact on the surface, preserved in the airless vacuum. Whether future astronauts could revive them with water is unknown. The crash triggered a formal reassessment of planetary protection protocols, raising the possibility that crashed spacecraft routinely seed target worlds with Earth organisms regardless of sterilization procedures. (Source: Nature, 2019)

☑ Which Fish Evolved a Biological Antifreeze by Repurposing a Digestive Enzyme Gene? Antarctic notothenioid fish inhabit water at 28.8 degrees F (-1.9 degrees C) — below the normal freezing point of vertebrate blood. Survival depends on antifreeze glycoproteins (AFGPs) that bind to ice crystals and block their growth. Their evolutionary origin is remarkable: these proteins arose from a segment encoding pancreatic trypsinogen. This digestive enzyme was repurposed into a structurally unrelated molecule performing a completely different biological function. Unlike chemical antifreeze, AFGPs do not lower the freezing point — they block crystal growth while leaving the phase transition temperature unchanged, a mechanism that has not been fully replicated artificially. (Source: PNAS, 2010)

☑ How Do Arctic Insects Freeze Completely Each Winter and Walk Away Unharmed in Spring? Many cold-climate insects produce thermal hysteresis proteins — antifreeze compounds that widen the gap between freezing and melting temperatures, permitting sub-zero survival without lethal ice formation. The spruce budworm produces proteins that suppress crystallization to around -30 degrees F (-34 degrees C). Arctic woolly bear moth caterpillars (Gynaephora groenlandica) in the Canadian High Arctic spend up to ten months of every year frozen solid, resume activity each summer, and repeat this freeze-thaw cycle for up to 14 years before completing metamorphosis — a larval development period longer than most small mammals live in their entire lifetimes. (Source: Journal of Experimental Biology, 1995)

☑ Which Fish Survives Months in Oxygen-Free Water by Excreting Alcohol Through Its Gills? The crucian carp (Carassius carassius) is the only vertebrate known to survive complete oxygen deprivation for months. In Nordic lakes sealed under winter ice, where all dissolved oxygen is consumed, it switches to anaerobic metabolism and produces ethanol as a waste product instead of lactic acid. Ethanol diffuses through the gills into the surrounding water, preventing the acid buildup that kills other vertebrates within minutes. Crucian carp under ice show blood ethanol levels of 50 mg per 100 ml — at or above the legal driving limit in many countries — yet suffer no measurable tissue damage. (Source: Scientific Reports, 2017)

☑ Can a Jellyfish Actually Reverse Its Own Aging and Return to Its Juvenile Form? The jellyfish Turritopsis dohrnii can, when stressed by starvation, injury, or aging, reverse its development entirely — transforming from a sexually mature medusa back into a juvenile polyp through transdifferentiation, in which differentiated adult cells revert to an unspecialized state and rebuild a new organism from scratch. This cycle has been repeated multiple times in laboratory individuals with no confirmed upper limit on reversals. It is not immortality: T. dohrnii is readily eaten by predators and killed by disease. What it possesses is a biological reset capability confirmed in no other multicellular animal. (Source: Biological Bulletin, 1996)

Together We Thrive

☑ Why Is the Naked Mole Rat the Only Mammal That Lives Like an Ant? The naked mole rat (Heterocephalus glaber) is the only mammal confirmed to be eusocial — a colony structure otherwise found only in insects. A single breeding queen suppresses reproduction in up to 300 workers through physical shoving and hormonal stress. Workers divide into castes: smaller individuals maintain tunnels and tend pups, while larger soldiers defend against snakes. If the queen dies, females fight — sometimes fatally — for succession. The winner's spine physically elongates to accommodate larger litters, a body transformation unique among mammals. (Source: PNAS, 1991)

☑ How Do 700,000 Army Ants Build a Living Bridge Using Nothing but Their Own Bodies? Army ants of the genus Eciton form bridges, ladders, and bivouacs entirely from interlocked living bodies. Workers grip each other's legs and mandibles, creating structures that shorten foraging routes across forest gaps. At night, up to 700,000 ants link into a bivouac — a hollow ball of living bodies sheltering the queen and brood at its core. No individual directs construction. The colony functions as a superorganism: collectively intelligent, individually simple, responding to local chemical cues that produce architecture no single ant can comprehend. (Source: PNAS, 2011)

☑ How Do Honeybees Vote on Where to Build Their Next Home? When a swarm needs a new nest site, scout bees inspect candidates independently, then return and perform waggle dances proportional to each site's quality. Better sites generate longer, more energetic dances, recruiting more scouts. Over hours, scouts visiting inferior sites gradually stop dancing, while supporters of the best site reach a quorum. The swarm lifts off only when a threshold number agrees on a single location — a democratic process studied by Thomas Seeley at Cornell that mirrors optimal group decision-making models in human organizations. (Source: Science, 2012)

☑ Did the Scientist Who Made the "Alpha Wolf" Famous Spend Decades Trying to Undo His Own Mistake? Wildlife biologist L. David Mech popularized the alpha wolf concept in his 1970 book, based on captive wolves forced into artificial groups. Decades of field research — much of it his own — revealed wild wolf packs are simply families: a breeding pair and their offspring from successive years. There are no dominance battles for rank because the "alphas" are the parents and the "subordinates" are their children. Mech formally requested that his publisher stop printing the original book. The correction took over 30 years to reach popular culture. (Source: Canadian Journal of Zoology, 1999)

☑ Why Would a Bat Vomit Blood Into the Mouth of an Unrelated Stranger? Common vampire bats (Desmodus rotundus) that fail to feed on a given night face starvation within 60 hours. Roost-mates that fed successfully regurgitate blood meals for hungry companions — even non-relatives. Gerald Wilkinson's landmark research showed bats track individual giving histories: those who refused to share when they had food were denied help when they later went hungry. The system operates as biological reciprocal altruism — cooperation enforced not by kinship but by memory-based scorekeeping across hundreds of interactions. (Source: Nature, 1984)

☑ Which Fish Cleans Inside a Shark's Open Mouth — and Lives to Do It Again? Bluestreak cleaner wrasse (Labroides dimidiatus) operate fixed "cleaning stations" on coral reefs, removing parasites and dead skin from visiting fish. Even predators that could swallow the wrasse in one bite — including moray eels and reef sharks — hold their mouths open and wait patiently. The wrasse prefers to eat nutritious client mucus, but cheating triggers client departure. Research showed that wrasse that cheat lose future clients, creating market-like incentive structures that maintain cooperation between species, with every reason to exploit each other. (Source: Nature, 2003)

☑ **Which Wild Bird Guides a Mammal to Honey — and Waits for Its Share?** The greater honeyguide (Indicator indicator) in sub-Saharan Africa actively leads honey badgers and human honey-hunters to wild bee colonies using a distinctive chattering flight. The bird cannot break into hives alone; the mammal cannot find them efficiently without the bird. After the hive is opened, the honeyguide feeds on beeswax it could not otherwise access. A 2016 field study in Mozambique confirmed that hunters following honeyguides found hives 54% more often than when searching alone, and the birds responded to specific human calls requesting guidance. (Source: Science, 2016)

☑ **Who Actually Hunts in a Lion Pride — and Why Doesn't the Hunter Eat First?** Females do nearly all hunting in African lion prides, coordinating ambush positions based on terrain and prey movement. Yet males eat first at every kill, consuming the richest portions before females and cubs can feed. This apparent injustice has a biological logic: males defend the pride's territory against rival coalitions — fights that are frequently fatal. Their survival depends on peak condition. Male coalitions of two to four brothers cooperate to hold territories spanning up to 100 square miles (259 sq km), and prides with stronger coalitions hold better hunting ground. (Source: Behavioral Ecology and Sociobiology, 1994)

☑ Is a Meerkat Sentinel Performing a Selfless Act — or Playing the Safest Card? Meerkat sentinels stand guard at elevated posts while others forage — seemingly sacrificing feeding time for the group's safety. Yet studies by Clutton-Brock's team at Cambridge revealed sentinels tend to begin guard duty only after they have fed well themselves. They are also closest to bolt holes and typically first to escape when a predator appears. The behavior looks altruistic but functions as low-cost insurance: a well-fed individual with the best escape route accepts minimal personal risk while gaining the indirect benefit of protecting close relatives who share its genes. (Source: Science, 1999)

☑ Which Insect Invented Agriculture 50 Million Years Before Humans Existed? Leafcutter ants of the tribe Attini do not eat the leaves they harvest. They carry leaf fragments underground, chew them into pulp, and feed the mulch to a fungus they cultivate in subterranean gardens. The fungus produces nutrient-rich nodules that the ants eat. Colonies of up to eight million workers maintain these gardens with antibiotics produced by bacteria living on their bodies, controlling pests in their crop. Fossil evidence dates this agricultural system to approximately 60 million years ago — making it the oldest known form of farming by any organism on Earth. (Source: PNAS, 2005)

☑ **How Does an Elephant Matriarch's Memory Save Her Family During Drought?** African elephant herds are led by the oldest female — the matriarch — whose accumulated knowledge of water sources, seasonal routes, and distant feeding grounds directly determines her family's survival. Research at Amboseli by Cynthia Moss showed that during the severe 1993 drought, families led by older matriarchs traveled to water sources they had not visited in decades, while herds with younger leaders suffered higher calf mortality. A matriarch's memory is, in measurable terms, her family's most valuable survival asset. (Source: Proceedings of the Royal Society B, 2001)

☑ **Why Does a Male Orca Stay With His Mother for His Entire Life?** In resident orca populations, neither males nor females leave their natal pod. Sons remain with their mothers until death — relationships lasting 50 years or more. A 2012 study found that when a mother died, her adult son's risk of dying within the following year increased by over eight times. Mothers share prey with adult sons, lead them to seasonal feeding grounds, and intervene in conflicts with other pods. No other large mammal male maintains such a lifelong, survival-critical bond with its mother beyond reproductive maturity. (Source: Science, 2012)

☑ **Can a Herd Protect You Just by Existing — Even if No One Is Watching Out for You?** In 1971, evolutionary biologist W. D. Hamilton proposed that animals cluster not from cooperation but from selfish geometry. Each moves toward the center of a group to place others between itself and a predator — a phenomenon he called the selfish herd. Mathematical models confirmed that the dilution effect alone reduces any individual's probability of being caught. A wildebeest in a herd of 1,000 faces roughly one-thousandth the predation risk of one standing alone — survival through arithmetic, requiring no coordination and no altruism whatsoever. (Source: Journal of Theoretical Biology, 1971)

☑ **What Mathematical Equation Explains Why an Animal Would Die for Its Relatives?** In 1964, W. D. Hamilton published a formula now known as Hamilton's Rule: an altruistic act will spread through a population when the cost to the actor is less than the benefit to the recipient multiplied by their genetic relatedness. A worker bee shares 75% of her genes with her sisters, making sacrificing her own reproduction to raise the queen's daughters genetically logical. This equation transformed biology by proving that self-sacrifice is not a paradox but a predictable outcome of natural selection operating on shared genes rather than individual survival. (Source: Journal of Theoretical Biology, 1964)

☑ Why Do a Coyote and a Badger Hunt Together — and Why Does It Actually Work? American badgers and coyotes have been documented hunting ground squirrels as a cooperative pair. The coyote chases prey above ground; the badger digs it out below. When hunting together, each animal's capture rate increases significantly because prey cannot escape in either direction. A 2020 trail camera video from a California wildlife crossing captured a coyote apparently waiting for a badger before both entered a culvert together — behavior suggesting the partnership involves active coordination, not mere coincidence of location. (Source: Journal of Mammalogy, 1992)

☑ Which Ants Run a Livestock Operation — Complete With Herding, Milking, and Protection? Many ant species tend colonies of aphids the way humans tend dairy cattle. Ants stroke aphids with their antennae to stimulate honeydew secretion, transport aphids to better feeding sites, and aggressively defend them against ladybugs and parasitoid wasps. Some species carry aphid eggs into their nests over winter and place the hatchlings on fresh shoots in spring. Chemical studies showed certain ants secrete substances from their feet that suppress aphid wing development — effectively preventing their livestock from flying away. (Source: Proceedings of the Royal Society B, 2007)

☑ **Why Would a Bird That Could Breed on Its Own Choose to Spend Years Helping Someone Else Raise Chicks?** Florida scrub jays delay their own reproduction for up to six years, remaining on their parents' territory as non-breeding helpers. Helpers defend the nest, mob predators, and feed nestlings. Research by Glen Woolfenden spanning over 30 years showed that breeding pairs with helpers fledged significantly more chicks than pairs without. Helpers gain experience, inherit quality territory when a parent dies, and increase the survival of siblings who carry their genes — making delayed reproduction a viable long-term strategy rather than a reproductive failure. (Source: American Naturalist, 1981)

☑ **Why Do Completely Unrelated Bird Species Travel, Feed, and Defend Territory Together?** Mixed-species foraging flocks — assemblages of chickadees, nuthatches, woodpeckers, and warblers moving as a coordinated unit through forest canopy — are among the most widespread cooperative phenomena in nature. Each species occupies a different foraging niche, reducing direct competition. The benefit is shared vigilance: more eyes detect predators sooner, allowing each individual to spend less time scanning and more time feeding. Studies in tropical forests found that species in mixed flocks increased their foraging efficiency by up to 30% compared to foraging alone. (Source: Behavioral Ecology, 2007)

☑ **What Does an Oxpecker Get From Sitting on a Buffalo — and Is the Buffalo Getting a Fair Deal?** Red-billed oxpeckers perch on large African mammals, feeding on ticks, blood-sucking flies, and dead skin. For decades, the relationship was described as textbook mutualism. Recent research complicated the picture: oxpeckers preferentially feed on blood from open wounds rather than ticks, sometimes enlarging wounds to access it. Yet host mammals tolerate them because oxpeckers also serve as alarm sentinels — their hissing calls warn hosts of approaching predators. The relationship sits on an unstable boundary between mutualism and parasitism, renegotiated continuously by both parties. (Source: Behavioral Ecology, 2000)

☑ How Does a Spotted Hyena Clan Decide Who Outranks Whom — and Why Does the Answer Surprise Biologists? Spotted hyena (Crocuta crocuta) clans of up to 130 individuals are led by a dominant female, and all females outrank all males. Rank is inherited matrilineally: a cub born to a high-ranking female immediately outranks all offspring of lower-ranking females, regardless of size. Males who disperse to new clans start at the absolute bottom. This female-dominated social hierarchy, with inherited rank and immigrant males holding no authority, more closely resembles some primate societies than any other carnivore system studied. (Source: Animal Behavior, 1996)

☑ Can Two Ravens Solve a Problem Together — and Then Split the Reward Fairly? In controlled experiments at the University of Vienna, ravens learned to simultaneously pull both ends of a rope to drag a food platform within reach — a task neither bird could complete alone. Pairs that cooperated successfully shared the reward without conflict. When researchers paired a cooperative raven with one that had previously stolen food, the cooperative bird refused to participate — remembering the cheat and withholding future partnership. Ravens track individual reputations across repeated social interactions and adjust cooperative investment accordingly. (Source: Current Biology, 2015)

☑ Does the Naked Mole Rat Queen Chemically Suppress Her Workers' Ability to Feel Pain? In naked mole rat colonies, workers show dramatically reduced sensitivity to certain chemical irritants compared to solitary mammals. Researchers discovered that a hormone cocktail in the queen's urine — the same signal that suppresses worker reproduction — also modulates pain perception in colony members. When queens were removed experimentally, workers' pain responses gradually returned to normal levels within weeks. The queen's chemical control extends beyond breeding rights into the basic sensory experience of her workforce — a degree of biological authority over others that has no parallel in any other mammalian society. (Source: Cell Reports, 2020)

☑ Why Do African Wild Dogs Take a Vote Before Every Hunt? Before a pack of African wild dogs (Lycaon pictus) departs on a hunt, members engage in a ritualized sneezing rally. Researchers at Botswana's Moremi Game Reserve found that a minimum number of sneezes — a quorum — must be reached before the group moves. Dominant individuals needed fewer supporting sneezes to trigger departure than subordinates did. This collective decision-making helps explain the species' extraordinary 80% hunting success rate, the highest of any large social predator — coordination begins before a single step is taken. (Source: Proceedings of the Royal Society B, 2017)

☑ **Which Insect Produces Soldiers Genetically Identical to Itself — Born Only to Die Defending the Colony?** Social aphids of the genus Pemphigus produce a specialized soldier caste through clonal reproduction. These soldiers are genetically identical to the aphids they protect. Armed with thickened forelegs and sharp stylets, they attack predators like ladybug larvae — often dying in the process. Because they are clones sharing 100% of their genes with nestmates, their sacrifice carries no genetic cost. It is altruism reduced to pure mathematics: the individual is expendable because every member of the colony carries the same genome. (Source: PNAS, 1992)

☑ **How Does a Termite Mound Maintain a Constant 86 Degrees F Inside While the Outside Air Swings by 50 Degrees?** Macrotermes termites in sub-Saharan Africa build mounds up to 17 feet (5.2 m) tall with internal ventilation shafts that regulate temperature at a near-constant 86 degrees F (30 degrees C) year-round. The colony cultivates a symbiotic fungus, Termitomyces, in underground gardens that require this precise temperature to produce the enzymes termites depend on for digestion. Workers constantly open and seal ventilation channels in response to external temperature shifts — a thermostat operated by thousands of individuals following local chemical cues with no central controller. (Source: Journal of Experimental Biology, 2001)

☑ **Why Do Birds From Completely Different Species Gang Up on a Predator Together?** When a songbird spots a perched hawk or owl, it issues a loud mobbing call that recruits not only its own species but neighboring species as well. Studies in European forests found that blackbirds, robins, wrens, and titmice converge simultaneously on a detected predator, diving and calling aggressively until it leaves. Each participant benefits from shared risk: a hawk confronted by 20 birds from five species is far less likely to ambush any one of them successfully. Interspecific mobbing is one of the most widespread cooperative defense systems in nature. (Source: Behavioral Ecology and Sociobiology, 2010)

☑ What Does It Take for a Chimpanzee to Build a Political Alliance That Lasts for Years? Male chimpanzees compete for alpha status not through brute strength alone but through strategic coalition-building, documented by Frans de Waal at Arnhem Zoo. Males invest hundreds of hours grooming specific allies, repay political support with mating access, and punish defectors by withdrawing grooming privileges. A physically weaker male can overthrow a stronger rival by securing the right alliances. De Waal observed coalitions lasting years, with members tracking debts and favors across dozens of interactions — a political system governed by reciprocity, memory, and calculated betrayal. (Source: Chimpanzee Politics, de Waal, 1982)

☑ How Does a Single Honeybee Queen Prevent 50,000 Workers From Reproducing? The queen honeybee secretes a pheromone blend called queen mandibular pheromone (QMP) that spreads through the hive via physical contact between workers. This chemical signal suppresses ovary development in every worker bee that receives it. If the queen dies or is removed, workers' ovaries begin developing within days, and some begin laying unfertilized eggs. QMP also inhibits workers from constructing queen cells — the large wax chambers needed to raise a replacement. A single chemical broadcast controls both the reproductive biology and the architectural behavior of an entire colony. (Source: Annual Review of Entomology, 2003)

☑ Which Partnership Pairs a Fish That Cannot Dig With a Shrimp That Cannot See? On Indo-Pacific coral reefs, goby fish and pistol shrimp form one of the most precisely divided labor partnerships in the animal kingdom. The nearly blind shrimp excavates and maintains a shared burrow while the sharp-eyed goby stands guard at the entrance. The shrimp maintains constant physical contact with the goby through its antenna. When the goby spots danger, a specific tail flick sends both animals into the burrow within a fraction of a second. Neither species thrives alone in predator-rich reef environments — survival depends on the other's complementary ability. (Source: Marine Biology, 2004)

☑ How Complex Is the Underground City Beneath a Prairie Dog Town? Black-tailed prairie dog (Cynomys ludovicianus) colonies — called towns — once stretched across hundreds of square miles of the American Great Plains. The largest recorded town in Texas in 1900 covered approximately 25,000 square miles (64,750 sq km) and housed an estimated 400 million animals. Tunnel systems include separate chambers for sleeping, nurseries, waste disposal, and listening posts near entrances. Families maintain distinct territorial boundaries called coteries within the town, and members greet each other with an open-mouthed "kiss" that confirms group membership through scent. (Source: Journal of Mammalogy, 2006)

☑ Is a Coral Reef Actually a City Built by Millions of Cooperating Species? Coral reefs house approximately 25% of all marine species despite covering less than 1% of the ocean floor. The structure itself is built by coral polyps hosting photosynthetic algae called zooxanthellae inside their tissues — a mutualism where the coral provides shelter and the algae provide up to 90% of the coral's energy through photosynthesis. Fish, sea urchins, and parrotfish control algae that would otherwise smother the coral. Cleaner shrimp remove parasites from reef fish. The system depends on hundreds of interlocking cooperative relationships, and removing any major participant can trigger cascading collapse. (Source: Science, 2003)

☑ Do Male Bottlenose Dolphins Form Political Alliances as Complex as Those of Chimpanzees? In Shark Bay, Australia, male bottlenose dolphins form nested alliances operating at three distinct levels. First-order alliances of two to three males cooperate to herd females. Second-order alliances of four to 14 males coordinate to steal females from rival groups or defend against such raids. Third-order alliances link second-order groups into larger networks that mobilize during major conflicts. Maintaining these relationships requires decades of social investment and individual recognition across hundreds of animals. It is the most complex multilevel alliance system documented outside humans. (Source: PNAS, 2022)

☑ Is the Damaraland Mole Rat Proof That Mammalian Eusociality Evolved More Than Once? For years, the naked mole rat stood alone as the only eusocial mammal. Then researchers confirmed that the Damaraland mole rat (Fukomys damarensis) of southern Africa also meets the strict criteria: a single breeding queen, non-breeding workers, and overlapping generations sharing a communal burrow. Unlike naked mole rats, Damaraland mole rats are fully furred and live in smaller colonies of up to 40 individuals. The discovery proved that the extraordinary leap to eusociality in mammals was not a one-time accident but an evolutionary pathway taken independently by at least two separate lineages. (Source: Journal of Zoology, 2000)

☑ **Why Do Musk Oxen Form a Circle With Their Calves in the Center When Wolves Attack?** When threatened by wolves, musk oxen instinctively arrange themselves into a defensive ring with adults facing outward and calves sheltered in the center. Each adult presents a wall of curved horns and a combined body mass that no wolf pack can breach. The formation is so effective that wolves typically abandon the attempt after testing the line. This cooperative defense evolved on open Arctic tundra where no cover exists — the herd itself becomes the fortress. The same strategy proved fatal when human hunters with rifles arrived, as the stationary circle made every animal an easy target. (Source: Canadian Journal of Zoology, 1988)

☑ **What Happens Inside a Beehive When a Worker Lays an Egg She Was Never Authorized to Produce?** In queenright honeybee colonies, workers occasionally attempt to lay unfertilized eggs that would develop into males. Other workers detect these rogue eggs — likely by chemical signature — and destroy them within hours. This behavior, called worker policing, was first documented by Francis Ratnieks at Cornell. Policing maintains the queen's reproductive monopoly because workers are more closely related to the queen's sons than to each other's sons. Genetic self-interest, not blind obedience, enforces the colony's reproductive order — making the hive a system where even rebellion is governed by mathematics. (Source: Nature, 1988)

☑ **Which Spiders Abandoned Solitary Life to Build Communal Webs Spanning Entire Trees?** Social spiders of the genus Anelosimus in South America construct communal webs stretching up to 16 feet (5 m) across, housing hundreds of individuals. Colony members cooperate in prey capture — subduing insects far larger than any individual could handle alone — and share food without aggression. Females collectively care for all young in the colony regardless of parentage. Fewer than 25 of the world's roughly 50,000 spider species have evolved this level of sociality, making cooperative spiders among the rarest social systems in the animal kingdom. (Source: Behavioral Ecology and Sociobiology, 2006)

☑ Is Grooming the Secret Currency That Governs Baboon Politics? In olive baboon troops, grooming is not merely hygiene — it is a transactional social tool with measurable returns. Baboons preferentially groom higher-ranking individuals and expect tolerance at feeding sites in return. When a female loses rank, her grooming network collapses within days as former partners redirect their attention upward. Robert Seyfarth and Dorothy Cheney at the University of Pennsylvania demonstrated that baboons track dozens of social relationships simultaneously, adjusting their grooming investments based on each partner's current rank and recent cooperative behavior toward them. (Source: Animal Behavior, 2009)

☑ How Do 5,000 Emperor Penguins Survive Antarctic Blizzards by Constantly Trading Places? During Antarctic winter storms with temperatures dropping to minus 76 degrees F (minus 60 degrees C) and winds exceeding 120 mph (193 km/h), male emperor penguins huddle in groups of up to 5,000 birds. The huddle is not static: individuals on the windward edge slowly shift inward while those at the warm center gradually rotate outward. Thermal imaging revealed interior temperatures reaching 99 degrees F (37 degrees C). The rotation ensures no individual bears the lethal outer position for long — survival through continuous, egalitarian movement that no single penguin directs. (Source: PLOS ONE, 2013)

☑ Why Did Eusociality Evolve So Many Times in Bees, Wasps, and Ants — but Almost Nowhere Else? The insect order Hymenoptera — bees, wasps, and ants — accounts for nearly every known eusocial species. The key lies in haplodiploidy: females develop from fertilized eggs and carry genes from both parents, while males develop from unfertilized eggs and carry only their mother's. This genetic system means sisters share 75% of their genes but only 50% with their own offspring. Raising sisters is genetically more rewarding than raising daughters — making the sacrifice of personal reproduction a mathematically favored strategy that has driven eusociality to evolve at least 12 times independently within this single order. (Source: Journal of Evolutionary Biology, 2008)

☑ Can Social Bonds in Pilot Whales Be So Strong That an Entire Pod Follows a Dying Member Onto Shore? Long-finned pilot whales are among the most frequently mass-stranded cetaceans worldwide. Their social bonds are exceptionally tight: pods of 20 to 100 individuals stay together for life, and members respond immediately to distress calls from any pod member. When a sick or disoriented whale swims into shallow water, others follow rather than abandon it. Rescuers who successfully refloat stranded pilot whales report that released individuals often turn back toward shore if other pod members remain beached — choosing social cohesion over personal survival. (Source: Marine Mammal Science, 2005)

☑ Can a Colony of Fire Ants Build a Raft Out of Its Own Members in Under Two Minutes? When floodwaters rise, red imported fire ants (Solenopsis invicta) link their bodies into a waterproof raft within 100 seconds. Workers grip each other's legs using adhesive pads on their feet, trapping air pockets that provide buoyancy. The raft can carry the queen, brood, and thousands of workers downstream for weeks. Georgia Institute of Technology researchers found the structure behaves as both a solid and a liquid — deforming around obstacles but never breaking apart. No individual ant can float, yet the collective is unsinkable. (Source: PNAS, 2011)

How Animals Shape Their World

☑ What Happened to Yellowstone When Wolves Disappeared for 70 Years — and What Happened When They Came Back? After wolves were eradicated from Yellowstone in 1926, elk populations exploded and overgrazed riverbank willows and aspens for decades, stripping the landscape. When 31 wolves were reintroduced in 1995, elk began avoiding exposed valleys where they were vulnerable. Within a decade, willow and aspen regenerated along streams, beaver colonies returned to build dams in the recovering waterways, songbird populations climbed, and the entire food web restructured itself — a textbook trophic cascade triggered by a single predator's return. (Source: Ecological Monographs, 2011)

☑ How Did Wolves Physically Change the Course of Yellowstone's Rivers? As wolves drove elk away from riverbanks, recovering willows and aspens stabilized eroding streambanks with dense root networks. Channels that had been wide, shallow, and prone to wandering became narrower and deeper. Erosion rates dropped measurably along monitored stretches. Geomorphologists documented that rivers began holding their courses more firmly within a few years, not through any direct engineering, but because a predator's presence allowed plants to anchor the soil that rivers flow through. The wolves never touched a riverbank, yet they reshaped the hydrology of an entire national park. (Source: Earth Surface Processes and Landforms, 2018)

☑ Why Does an Entire Coastal Ecosystem Collapse When Sea Otters Disappear? Sea otters eat sea urchins, keeping their populations in check. When fur traders hunted otters to near extinction in the 18th and 19th centuries, urchin populations exploded unchecked. They consumed vast kelp forests down to bare rock — creating desolate seascapes called urchin barrens. Where otters later recovered, kelp forests regrew within just a few years, restoring habitat for hundreds of fish and invertebrate species that depend on kelp canopy for shelter, food, and nursery grounds. One predator's appetite holds the entire system together. (Source: Science, 1974)

☑ Which Scientist Proved That Removing One Species Can Destroy an Entire Ecosystem — by Throwing Starfish Off a Rock? In 1963, ecologist Robert Paine removed every predatory starfish Pisaster ochraceus from a tidal stretch in Washington State and monitored what happened. Within months, mussels monopolized the rock surface and crowded out 15 other species. The adjacent control area, where starfish remained, kept its full diversity. The experiment coined the term "keystone species" — an organism whose impact on its community is disproportionately large relative to its own abundance — and it fundamentally changed how ecologists understand biodiversity. (Source: The American Naturalist, 1966)

☑ How Do Elephants Create Water Sources That Hundreds of Other Species Depend On? African elephants dig into dry riverbeds using their tusks and feet, reaching subsurface water that no other savanna animal can access. These excavations become critical water holes during droughts, sustaining zebras, wildebeest, baboons, and dozens of bird species. By felling large trees and stripping bark, elephants also convert dense woodland into open grassland — maintaining the mosaic savanna structure that supports Africa's extraordinary mammal diversity. Remove elephants, and forests close in, water holes vanish, and the entire savanna community contracts. (Source: African Journal of Ecology, 2004)

☑ Can a 40-Pound Rodent Reshape an Entire Landscape More Effectively Than Heavy Machinery? Beavers build dams that create wetlands, raise water tables, and slow flood pulses across entire watersheds. A single beaver dam can raise the local water table by up to 5 feet (1.5 m) and increase plant species diversity by 33% in the surrounding floodplain. Their ponds store carbon, filter sediment, and provide breeding habitat for amphibians, fish, waterfowl, and insects. Beavers once numbered over 100 million in North America alone — making them among the most influential ecosystem engineers the continent has ever produced. (Source: BioScience, 2018)

☑ **Which Two Species Have Been Locked in a Mutual Dependency for 34 Million Years — and Would Both Go Extinct Without the Other?** Fig trees and fig wasps represent one of the longest known obligate mutualisms. Its own species-specific wasp pollinates each of the roughly 750 fig species. The wasp enters a fig, pollinates the flowers, lays eggs inside some of them, and dies. Her offspring hatch, mate, and carry pollen to the next fig. Neither organism can reproduce without the other — a partnership older than the Himalayas that sustains tropical ecosystems, since figs are a keystone food source for hundreds of bird and mammal species. (Source: Annual Review of Ecology, Evolution, and Systematics, 2008)

☑ **Which Beetle Removes 80% of Livestock Dung From Some Pastures — and Saves the Cattle Industry Billions?** Dung beetles bury animal waste underground at remarkable speed, aerating soil, recycling nitrogen, and suppressing parasitic fly larvae that breed in surface dung. Australia, which had no native dung beetles adapted to cattle waste, imported 23 African and European species beginning in 1967 to process the millions of cattle dung pats accumulating on its pastures. The economic benefit to Australia's cattle industry alone has been estimated at over $1 billion annually in reduced parasite burden, improved soil fertility, and increased pasture growth. (Source: Biological Conservation, 2016)

☑ What Happened to the Northwest Atlantic When Humans Removed the Cod? The collapse of the Atlantic cod fishery off Newfoundland in 1992 did not simply reduce one fish population — it restructured an entire marine ecosystem from the top down. With cod removed, their prey species exploded: northern shrimp and snow crab populations surged to fill the vacuum. Smaller forage fish declined under altered predation pressures. Three decades later, cod have still not recovered to their former numbers, and the ecosystem has settled into a fundamentally different configuration that scientists believe may now be self-sustaining without intervention. (Source: Canadian Journal of Fisheries and Aquatic Sciences, 2005)

☑ Why Do Coral Reefs Support 25% of All Marine Species on Less Than 1% of the Ocean Floor? Coral reefs are built by tiny polyps that secrete calcium carbonate skeletons over centuries, creating three-dimensional structures of extraordinary complexity. Symbiotic algae called zooxanthellae live inside coral tissue, providing up to 90% of the coral's energy through photosynthesis in exchange for shelter and nutrients. When ocean temperatures rise just 1–2 degrees C above the seasonal maximum, corals expel these algae in a stress response called bleaching — stripping the reef of its primary energy source and threatening to collapse the most biodiverse marine habitat on Earth. (Source: Science, 2007)

☑ How Much of the World's Food Supply Depends on Animals Most People Barely Notice? Approximately 75% of the world's leading food crops depend to some degree on animal pollinators — primarily bees, but also butterflies, moths, beetles, bats, and birds. The economic value of pollination services has been estimated at $235–577 billion per year globally. Coffee, almonds, cocoa, and most fruit crops would produce dramatically reduced yields without pollinator visits. A sustained collapse in pollinator populations would threaten global food production on a scale that no existing agricultural technology could adequately replace. (Source: IPBES Global Assessment, 2019)

☑ Why Do More Than 150 Animal Species Depend on a Burrowing Rodent for Their Survival? Black-tailed prairie dog colonies create underground tunnel networks that aerate compacted soil, channel rainwater downward, and increase nitrogen content in surrounding vegetation. Burrowing owls, black-footed ferrets, rattlesnakes, and over 150 other species use prairie dog burrows for shelter, nesting, or hunting grounds. The clipped grassland around colonies attracts pronghorn and bison, which prefer the shorter, more nutritious growth. When colonies are eliminated, these dependent species decline or vanish entirely — confirming the prairie dog as a keystone of the Great Plains ecosystem. (Source: Conservation Biology, 2006)

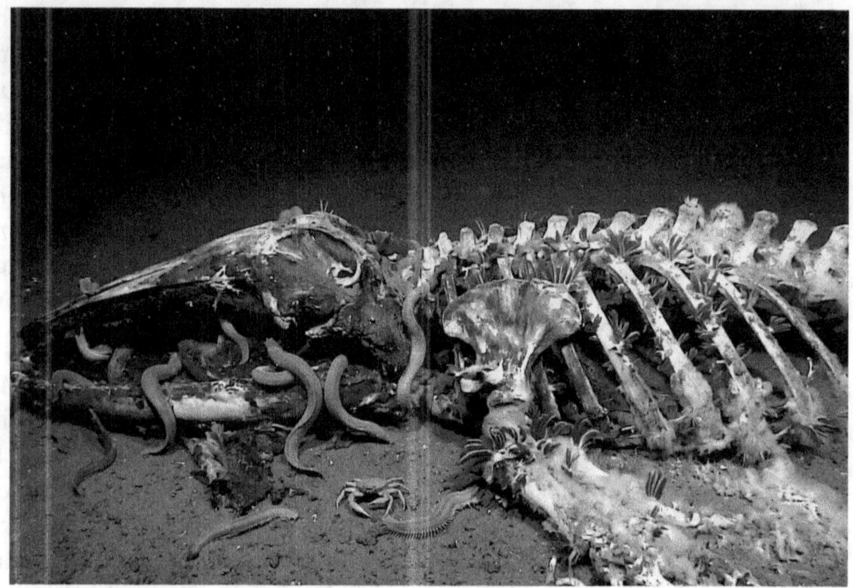

☑ How Does a Dead Whale Feed an Entire Deep-Sea Community for 50 Years? When a great whale dies and sinks to the ocean floor, its carcass — called a whale fall — becomes a self-contained ecosystem in the otherwise food-scarce deep sea. Over 400 species have been documented feeding on a single whale fall, from hagfish and sleeper sharks in the scavenging stage to bone-eating Osedax worms and chemosynthetic bacteria that extract energy from lipids locked inside whale bones. The succession of communities on a single carcass can sustain life for over 50 years in total darkness. (Source: Deep-Sea Research Part I, 2010)

☑ Did Entire Forests Move Hundreds of Miles Northward After the Ice Age — Carried by Animals? When glaciers retreated roughly 12,000 years ago, trees could not simply relocate to newly available land. Animals carried them. Jays cached acorns miles beyond parent oaks. Bears deposited berry seeds in distant feces. Squirrels buried nuts that they never retrieved. Studies of post-glacial pollen records show that oak forests advanced northward at rates far exceeding what wind dispersal alone could explain — up to 1,600 feet (500 m) per year in some regions. The expansion of temperate forests was driven almost entirely by animal seed dispersal. (Source: Annual Review of Ecology and Systematics, 2000)

☑ What Happened in India When 99% of Its Vultures Died Within a Decade? Between the 1990s and early 2000s, India's vulture population collapsed by over 99% after livestock were widely treated with the anti-inflammatory drug diclofenac, which proved lethal to vultures feeding on treated carcasses. Without vultures to consume dead animals, rotting livestock accumulated across the landscape. Feral dog populations surged to exploit the new food source — and with them, rabies cases spiked. Researchers estimated that approximately 50,000 additional human deaths from rabies resulted from the vulture collapse. A single missing scavenger triggered a public health catastrophe. (Source: Ecological Economics, 2014)

☑ **Is There an Animal That Transports Thousands of Tons of Nutrients From Land to Water Every Single Day?** Hippos graze on land at night and defecate in rivers during the day, transferring an estimated 800 metric tons of silicon into Africa's Mara River watershed annually. This silicon is essential for diatoms — microscopic algae that form the base of aquatic food webs and produce a significant share of the oxygen in freshwater systems. Researchers found that hippo-derived nutrients fundamentally alter river chemistry downstream and sustain aquatic ecosystems that would otherwise be nutrient-poor and far less productive. (Source: Science Advances, 2018)

☑ **Can a Single Oyster Really Filter 50 Gallons of Water Every Day?** An adult Eastern oyster filters approximately 50 gallons (190 liters) of water daily, removing algae, sediment, and excess nitrogen as it feeds. Before industrial-scale harvesting began, Chesapeake Bay's oyster population could filter the entire bay's water volume in under a week. Today, with oyster populations reduced by over 85%, that same filtration takes over a year — contributing directly to the algal blooms and oxygen-depleted dead zones that now plague the bay every summer. Oyster reef restoration projects aim to rebuild this lost biological filtration capacity. (Source: Marine Ecology Progress Series, 2004)

☑ **Which Fish Creates the White Sand Beaches That Tropical Tourism Depends On?** Parrotfish bite chunks of coral with fused beak-like teeth, digest the photosynthetic algae growing within, and excrete the calcium carbonate skeleton as fine white sand. A single large humphead parrotfish can produce over 800 pounds (360 kg) of sand per year. The iconic white beaches of Hawaii, the Caribbean, and the Maldives are composed substantially of parrotfish excrement — biogenic sediment accumulated over thousands of years of continuous coral grazing. Without parrotfish, these beaches would erode faster than they are replenished. (Source: Marine Ecology Progress Series, 2010)

☑ **Why Is a Dead Tree With Holes in It One of the Most Valuable Structures in a Forest?** Woodpeckers excavate nest cavities in standing dead trees that are subsequently used by over 40 bird and mammal species incapable of creating their own holes — including screech owls, American kestrels, flying squirrels, and wood ducks. Without woodpecker activity, these cavity-nesting species lose critical breeding habitat. A single pileated woodpecker excavation can serve successive tenants for over a decade after the woodpecker moves on, making woodpeckers quiet architects of biodiversity across temperate and boreal forests worldwide. (Source: The Condor: Ornithological Applications, 2002)

☑ What Happens to an Ecosystem When Its Largest Predators Are Systematically Removed? Scientists call it trophic downgrading — the cascading deterioration of an ecosystem following the loss of its top predators. Without wolves, elk overgraze riverbanks. Without sharks, mid-level predators multiply unchecked and deplete smaller fish populations. Without big cats, herbivores reshape entire forests. A landmark 2011 review examined ecosystems across all six vegetated continents and found the same pattern everywhere: removing apex predators destabilizes the entire food web below them, often triggering irreversible changes within a single decade of the predator's disappearance. (Source: Science, 2011)

☑ What Role Did Three Billion Passenger Pigeons Play in North American Forests — and What Did Those Forests Lose When Every Bird Was Gone? At their peak, passenger pigeons numbered roughly 3 billion and traveled in flocks so vast they darkened skies for hours. Massive flocks consumed billions of acorns, beechnuts, and chestnuts, creating intense disturbance cycles that opened forest canopy gaps and allowed sun-loving plants to regenerate. When the species went extinct in 1914, forests lost their most powerful natural mechanism for large-scale mast consumption — and many ecologists believe the resulting shift toward closed-canopy dominance permanently altered the composition of eastern North American woodlands. (Source: Ecological Monographs, 2017)

☑ Why Did Charles Darwin Spend the Last 40 Years of His Life Obsessed With Earthworms? Darwin's final book, published in 1881, argued that earthworms were among the most important animals in the history of the world. He was right. Earthworms process between 10 and 36 tons of soil per acre per year, turning over entire topsoil layers, aerating compacted ground, and breaking down organic matter into nutrient-rich castings that plants absorb directly. Modern soil science has confirmed that earthworm activity increases nitrogen availability by up to 25% and water infiltration rates by as much as six times in the soils they inhabit. (Source: Soil Biology and Biochemistry, 2004)

☑ **How Do Dead Salmon Feed Forests That Stand Miles From the Nearest Stream?** Pacific salmon carry marine-derived nutrients — nitrogen, phosphorus, and carbon accumulated over years at sea — upstream into freshwater systems. When bears, eagles, and other predators drag salmon carcasses into the forest, those nutrients enter the soil directly. Trees growing within 500 feet (150 m) of salmon-bearing streams in the Pacific Northwest contain measurably higher concentrations of marine-derived nitrogen in their growth rings. Scientists have documented that up to 24% of the nitrogen in streamside vegetation originated in the ocean and was delivered exclusively by spawning salmon. (Source: Ecosystems, 2001)

☑ **How Do Whales Fertilize the Ocean by Doing Nothing More Than Swimming to the Surface to Breathe?** Whales feed at depth and defecate near the surface, releasing iron-rich fecal plumes into sunlit waters where phytoplankton can use them. This nutrient transfer — called the "whale pump" — stimulates phytoplankton blooms that absorb carbon dioxide and form the base of marine food webs. Researchers in the Southern Ocean estimated that sperm whales alone transport approximately 50 metric tons of iron to the surface annually through their feces, stimulating enough phytoplankton growth to absorb an additional 400,000 metric tons of carbon each year. (Source: Proceedings of the Royal Society B, 2010)

☑ What Happens to an Entire Ocean Ecosystem When Sharks Are Removed From the Top of the Food Chain? Off the eastern coast of the United States, the systematic decline of large shark populations triggered a cascade that restructured coastal waters. Without sharks controlling them, populations of cownose rays surged to an estimated 40 million. Those rays consumed nearly all the bay scallops in North Carolina's waters, collapsing a century-old commercial fishery by 2004. Parallel studies worldwide have documented similar cascades — shark declines followed by explosions in jellyfish, algal overgrowth, and the loss of commercially important shellfish species across multiple ocean basins. (Source: Science, 2007)

☑ Why Are Mussel Beds Some of the Most Important Geological Structures Built by Any Living Animal? Blue mussels anchor themselves in dense aggregations on exposed coastlines, forming reefs that absorb up to 60% of incoming wave energy before it reaches the shoreline. These living structures trap sediment, slow erosion, and create sheltered microhabitats where hundreds of invertebrate and algal species thrive. In the Wadden Sea alone — a UNESCO World Heritage site along the coasts of the Netherlands, Germany, and Denmark — mussel beds stabilize enormous stretches of intertidal mudflat that would otherwise erode under storm-driven wave action within a single season. (Source: Marine Ecology Progress Series, 2009)

☑ Can a Single Little Brown Bat Eat 1,000 Mosquitoes in a Single Hour? Yes — and the agricultural implications are staggering. Little brown bats consume roughly 1,000 mosquito-sized insects per hour during peak feeding, and a maternity colony of 150 bats can eat over 1.3 million insects in a single summer night. When white-nose syndrome devastated bat populations across eastern North America beginning in 2006, scientists estimated the lost pest-control services alone cost American agriculture $3.7 billion per year in increased pesticide use and crop damage — making bats one of the most economically valuable wild animals on the continent. (Source: Science, 2011)

☑ What Is the Annual Economic Value of Insect-Eating Birds to the World's Farmers? A 2018 global analysis estimated that insectivorous birds provide between $49 billion and $104 billion annually in pest-suppression services to agriculture worldwide. In Costa Rican coffee plantations, farms with healthy bird populations experienced 50% less damage from the coffee berry borer — the crop's most destructive pest. In apple orchards across Europe, bird predation reduced caterpillar damage so effectively that researchers measured a direct increase in fruit quality and yield on farms that installed nest boxes compared with identical orchards that did not. (Source: Biological Reviews, 2018)

☑ How Did 102 Cane Toads Released in Australia in 1935 Become 200 Million — and What Have They Destroyed? Australia imported cane toads from Hawaii to control sugarcane beetles, but the toads ignored the beetles and spread across the continent at up to 37 miles (60 km) per year. Their skin secretes bufotoxin, lethal to nearly every native predator that attempts to eat them — including quolls, freshwater crocodiles, and monitor lizards, all of which suffered severe population crashes after cane toad arrival. The invasion front now spans the entire tropical north, and native predator populations have not recovered across hundreds of thousands of square miles. (Source: Biological Conservation, 2009)

☑ How Did a Pet-Trade Snake Quietly Erase 90% of the Mammals From a National Park? Burmese pythons, released or escaped from pet owners in the 1980s, established a breeding population in Florida's Everglades and multiplied explosively in a subtropical habitat with abundant prey and no natural predators. By 2012, surveys documented declines of 99% in raccoons, 98.9% in opossums, and 87.5% in bobcats across areas where pythons had been established longest. The pythons have fundamentally restructured the Everglades mammal community in under three decades — a pace of faunal collapse that ecologists describe as unprecedented for a single invasive predator. (Source: Proceedings of the National Academy of Sciences, 2012)

☑ What Happened After 60 European Starlings Were Released in New York City in 1890? In 1890, a Shakespeare enthusiast named Eugene Schieffelin released approximately 60 European starlings in Central Park as part of an effort to introduce every bird mentioned in Shakespeare's works to America. Within 60 years, the population had expanded coast to coast. Starlings now outcompete native cavity-nesting birds — including bluebirds, woodpeckers, and purple martins — for limited nest sites, and their enormous roosting flocks damage grain crops to the tune of roughly $800 million per year in agricultural losses across the United States. (Source: Annual Review of Ecology and Systematics, 2003)

☑ Which Beetle Depends Entirely on Forest Fires for Its Survival — and Arrives at a Blaze Before the Firefighters? The black fire beetle Melanophila acuminata has infrared sensors on its thorax that detect forest fires from over 50 miles (80 km) away. It flies directly toward the blaze because freshly burned trees, still too hot for any other insect, are the only place where it lays its eggs. Its larvae feed on fire-killed wood with no competition. The beetle is one of more than 50 insect species in North America classified as obligate pyrophiles — organisms that literally cannot complete their life cycles without wildfire. (Source: Journal of Insect Science, 2012)

☑ **What Are "Ecological Ghosts" — and Why Do Some Fruits Still Grow for Animals That Went Extinct 10,000 Years Ago?** Avocados, Osage oranges, and honey locust pods all produce large, fleshy fruits encasing tough seeds — yet no living animal in their native range disperses them effectively. These fruits evolved to be eaten by Pleistocene megafauna: giant ground sloths, gomphotheres, and mastodons that swallowed them whole and deposited seeds miles away. When those animals went extinct roughly 10,000 years ago, the plants lost their dispersal partners. Still, they kept producing fruit for consumers that no longer exist — a phenomenon ecologists call anachronistic dispersal syndrome. (Source: Proceedings of the National Academy of Sciences, 2009)

☑ **Why Are Vanishing Frogs One of the Most Alarming Warning Signs in Modern Ecology?** Amphibians breathe partly through their skin, absorbing water and dissolved gases directly from their environment — making them exceptionally sensitive to chemical contamination, UV radiation, and temperature change. Since the 1980s, over 200 amphibian species have gone extinct or are suspected of extinction worldwide, and 41% of all remaining amphibian species are now classified as threatened. Because frogs respond to environmental degradation faster than almost any other vertebrate group, ecologists use amphibian population trends as real-time bioindicators — living early-warning systems for ecosystem health. (Source: IUCN Global Amphibian Assessment, 2022)

☑ **Why Is a Hole Dug by an Alligator One of the Most Critical Structures in the Florida Everglades?** American alligators excavate deep depressions called "gator holes" in the limestone bedrock of the Everglades. During the dry season, when surrounding marshes evaporate, these pools become the last available freshwater for miles. Fish, turtles, wading birds, snails, and dozens of invertebrate species concentrate in and around gator holes, creating dense refugia that sustain entire local food webs until the rains return. Without alligator engineering, dry-season mortality among freshwater species across the Everglades would increase dramatically. (Source: Ecological Engineering, 2012)

☑ **How Does Seabird Excrement Fertilize Entire Island Ecosystems From the Ground Up?** Seabird guano is extraordinarily rich in nitrogen and phosphorus — concentrated nutrients that birds absorb from marine prey and deposit on land at nesting colonies. On islands where seabird populations remain intact, guano enriches soils so substantially that coral reefs adjacent to bird colonies grow at rates up to 50% faster than reefs near seabird-free islands, fueled by nutrient runoff. Researchers studying islands in the Indian Ocean found that removing invasive rats — which had decimated seabird colonies — restored guano-driven nutrient cycling that measurably improved reef fish biomass within just a few years. (Source: Nature, 2018)

☑ **What happens to a Seagrass Meadow When the Animals That Graze It Disappear?** Green sea turtles and dugongs graze seagrass beds in a pattern that prevents any single species of seagrass from monopolizing the meadow, maintaining biodiversity and promoting new growth. Where overhunting has removed these grazers, seagrass meadows accumulate dense mats of dead material, light penetration drops, and meadow health declines. Seagrass ecosystems store carbon up to 35 times faster per unit area than tropical rainforests — making the animals that maintain them unexpectedly important players in global carbon sequestration and climate regulation. (Source: Nature Geoscience, 2012)

☑ **Why Do Tens of Millions of Bison Once Matter More to the Great Plains Than Any Fence or Plow?** Before European settlement, an estimated 30 to 60 million American bison maintained the Great Plains grassland through three interlocking behaviors: grazing that prevented woody plant encroachment, wallowing that created shallow depressions trapping rainwater and supporting wetland plants, and trampling that broke soil crusts and pressed seeds into the ground. Tallgrass prairie ecologists have documented that bison-grazed areas support up to 60% more plant species than ungrazed areas, because bison preferentially eat dominant grasses and create space for rarer wildflowers and forbs to grow. (Source: BioScience, 2019)

☑ Why Are Mangrove Forests — Rooted in Salt Water — Among the Most Productive Ecosystems on the Planet? Mangrove root systems create dense underwater labyrinths that serve as nursery habitat for an estimated 75% of commercially harvested tropical fish species at some life stage. The tangled roots trap sediment, buffer coastlines against storm surges, and store up to four times more carbon per acre than terrestrial tropical forests. Despite this ecological and economic value — estimated at over $33,000 per hectare annually in coastal protection services alone — the world has lost roughly 35% of its mangrove forests since 1980, primarily to shrimp farming and coastal development. (Source: Annual Review of Marine Science, 2014)

☑ Which Slow-Moving Ocean-Floor Animal Quietly Processes More Sediment Than Any Other Group of Deep-Sea Organisms? Sea cucumbers dominate the deep-sea floor in many regions, making up over 90% of total animal biomass at depths below 13,000 feet (4,000 m). They vacuum organic matter from sediment, digest it, and excrete processed material that other organisms can use — a process called bioturbation. In some abyssal regions, sea cucumbers rework the entire top layer of ocean-floor sediment once every few years, cycling nutrients and oxygen through deposits that would otherwise become biologically stagnant. Remove them, and the deep-sea nutrient cycle slows measurably. (Source: Deep-Sea Research Part II, 2003)

The Record Books

☑ Is the Blue Whale the Largest Animal That Has Ever Lived on Earth? Yes — and not by a small margin. The blue whale reaches lengths of 100 feet (30.5 m) and weights of 200 tons (181 metric tons), exceeding every dinosaur whose mass has been reliably estimated. No fossil record from any era contains an animal approaching this size. The blue whale's tongue alone weighs as much as an adult elephant, and a single calf gains roughly 200 pounds (91 kg) per day during its first year of life. The ocean's buoyancy is the only reason a skeleton can support this body at all. (Source: NOAA Fisheries)

☑ How Does the Largest Heart on Earth Beat Slowly Enough to Hear Individual Thumps? The blue whale's heart is the size of a small car and weighs approximately 400 pounds (181 kg). During deep dives, its heartbeat drops to as few as two beats per minute, then surges to 37 beats per minute when the whale surfaces to breathe. Stanford University researchers recorded this range for the first time in 2019 using suction-cup sensors attached to a free-diving whale off the California coast. Each contraction pumps roughly 58 gallons (220 liters) of blood through an aorta wide enough for a human toddler to crawl through. (Source: Stanford University, 2019)

☑ **Which Mammal Weighs Less Than a Penny and Has a Heart That Beats 25 Times Per Second?** The Etruscan shrew (Suncus etruscus) holds the record for the smallest mammal by weight at just 0.06 oz (1.8 g) — lighter than a single US penny. Despite this minuscule size, its heart rate reaches 1,500 beats per minute, the fastest of any mammal. This extraordinary metabolic rate means the shrew must consume roughly 1.5 to two times its own body weight in food each day or die within hours. Found across southern Europe and parts of Asia, it hunts insects with rapid, precise strikes powered entirely by this relentless internal engine. (Source: Journal of Mammalogy)

☑ **Can an Insect Weigh More Than Most Birds?** The giant weta (Deinacrida heteracantha) of New Zealand holds the record as the heaviest insect on Earth, with documented specimens reaching 2.5 oz (71 g) — heavier than a house sparrow. Its enormous size is a textbook example of island gigantism, a phenomenon where species evolve larger body sizes in the absence of mammalian predators that would normally limit their survival. Before humans introduced rats and stoats to New Zealand, the weta occupied ecological niches typically filled by mice. Today, the species is critically endangered, surviving primarily on predator-free offshore islands. (Source: Victoria University, New Zealand)

☑ **Where Was the Smallest Vertebrate on Earth Hiding Until 2009?** Paedophryne amauensis, a frog no larger than a housefly, measures just 0.27 inches (7.7 mm) in body length — the smallest vertebrate ever recorded. Researchers discovered it in the leaf litter of Papua New Guinea's tropical rainforest, where its high-pitched insect-like call had been mistaken for that of an actual insect for years. Unlike most frogs, it skips the tadpole stage entirely, hatching directly as a miniature adult. Its discovery pushed the vertebrate size record below the previous holder, a tiny Indonesian fish, and demonstrated that tropical leaf litter still conceals unknown species. (Source: PLOS ONE, 2012)

☑ **Which Bird Builds a Nest the Size of Half a Walnut Shell?** The bee hummingbird (Mellisuga helenae), found only in Cuba, is the smallest bird on Earth at 2.2 inches (5.6 cm) long and 0.07 oz (2 g) in weight. Its nest, woven from cobwebs and bark, is barely half the size of a walnut shell, holding eggs no larger than coffee beans. Despite its size, the bee hummingbird beats its wings up to 80 times per second — so fast the motion is invisible to the human eye — and its iridescent plumage shifts between blue, green, and red depending on the angle of sunlight. (Source: Cornell Lab of Ornithology)

☑ **How Did Scientists Determine That a Clam Born During the Ming Dynasty Lived to 507 Years Old?** In 2006, researchers at Bangor University dredged an ocean quahog clam (Arctica islandica) from the seabed off Iceland. They counted 507 annual growth rings in its shell — making it the longest-lived individual animal ever confirmed. Nicknamed "Ming" after the Chinese dynasty in power when it was born around 1499, the clam was accidentally killed when its shell was opened for analysis. Radiocarbon dating later verified the ring count. Ocean quahogs deposit one visible band each year, functioning as a biological calendar that records both age and ocean conditions of each season. (Source: Bangor University, 2006)

☑ **What Can a Clam's Growth Rings Tell Scientists About Centuries of Ocean History?** The growth rings that revealed the ocean quahog's 507-year lifespan also function as a detailed environmental archive. Each ring's width and chemical composition record the water temperature, salinity, and nutrient conditions of the year it formed — a field called sclerochronology. By cross-referencing rings from living and dead shells, researchers have reconstructed continuous ocean climate records spanning over 1,000 years for the North Atlantic. These biological archives have confirmed volcanic cooling events, shifts in ocean circulation, and multi-decade climate cycles that no instrument was present to measure at the time. (Source: Geology, 2013)

☑ Which Animal Produces a Sound Louder Than a Saturn V Rocket at Close Range? The sperm whale generates clicks measured at 236 dB — the loudest sound produced by any living animal. A jet engine at full thrust registers roughly 150 dB, and a Saturn V rocket at 100 feet (30.5 m) measured approximately 204 dB. Because the decibel scale is logarithmic, the sperm whale's click is not slightly louder but exponentially more powerful than either. The whale produces this sound by forcing air through oil-filled chambers in its massive head, focusing the click into a narrow beam used for echolocation in the lightless deep ocean. (Source: Madsen et al., 2002)

☑ Why Does the Sperm Whale Need the Most Powerful Biological Sonar on Earth? Sperm whales hunt giant squid and other prey at depths exceeding 3,280 feet (1,000 m), where no sunlight penetrates. Their 236 dB echolocation clicks travel through water at nearly 5,000 feet (1,524 m) per second and bounce off objects up to 1,600 feet (488 m) away, returning detailed acoustic images of size, shape, and movement. The whale's spermaceti organ — a waxy, oil-filled structure that can weigh over 2,000 pounds (907 kg) — acts as an acoustic lens, focusing sound energy into a precise beam. No artificial sonar system of comparable size matches its range-to-power ratio. (Source: Journal of the Acoustical Society of America, 2006)

☑ What Makes the Three-Toed Sloth the Slowest Mammal on Earth — by a Wide Margin? The three-toed sloth moves at a ground speed of 0.15 mph (0.24 km/h), making it the slowest mammal ever measured. At this pace, it would take 17 hours to cover a single mile. In the trees, it moves only slightly faster, spending up to 20 hours a day motionless. Its metabolic rate is the lowest of any non-hibernating mammal — roughly 40% lower than expected for its body size. The sloth's entire physiology, from low muscle mass to slow digestion, is calibrated for maximum energy conservation in a canopy where competition for leaves is minimal. (Source: Smithsonian Tropical Research Institute)

☑ Why Did Evolution Strip Speed From an Entire Lineage of Mammals? The sloth's extreme slowness is not a design flaw but a refined survival strategy that has persisted for over 30 million years. By eating low-calorie leaves that most other mammals reject and moving so slowly that predators relying on motion detection frequently overlook them, sloths occupy a niche with almost no competitors. Their body temperature fluctuates with the environment — unusual for a mammal — further reducing energy demands. Ground sloths that went extinct roughly 10,000 years ago weighed up to four tons (3.6 metric tons), proving the lineage once included powerful species before evolving in the opposite direction. (Source: Proceedings of the Royal Society B, 2016)

☑ How Deep Can a Mammal Dive Before the Ocean Crushes It? The Cuvier's beaked whale holds the confirmed record for the deepest mammal dive at 9,816 feet (2,992 m) — nearly two miles below the surface. At that depth, water pressure exceeds 4,300 pounds per square inch (296 atmospheres), enough to crush a submarine not specifically engineered for extreme depth. Satellite-tagged whales in the study routinely dove beyond 6,500 feet (1,981 m), staying submerged for over two hours per dive. The record-setting individual remained underwater for approximately two hours and 18 minutes before resurfacing, having descended to a depth where no sunlight has reached for thousands of feet. (Source: PLOS ONE, 2014)

☑ What Happens Inside a Whale's Body During a Dive That Would Kill a Human in Minutes? When a Cuvier's beaked whale descends past 300 feet (91 m), its lungs collapse completely — a controlled structural failure that prevents nitrogen from dissolving into the blood and causing decompression sickness. Oxygen for the dive is stored not in the lungs but in hemoglobin-rich blood and myoglobin-saturated muscles, holding roughly three times the oxygen reserves of a comparable land mammal. The spleen contracts on descent, releasing stored oxygen-carrying red blood cells into circulation. Heart rate drops to as few as four beats per minute, directing blood exclusively to the brain and essential organs. (Source: Journal of Experimental Biology, 2018)

☑ Which Fish Outruns Every Other Animal in the Ocean — and Uses a Sail to Do It? The sailfish (Istiophorus platypterus) is the fastest fish in the ocean, clocked at 68 mph (110 km/h) in burst sprints. Its signature dorsal fin, which folds flat during high-speed chases, can be raised to form a sail-like barrier that herds smaller fish into tight, disoriented clusters. The sailfish's body is built for minimal drag: a pointed bill reduces water resistance, and crescent-shaped tail fins generate maximum thrust per stroke. Hunting groups take turns slashing through bait balls with their bills at full speed. (Source: FAO Species Catalog)

☑ How Large Is the World's Biggest Spider — and Why Does It Hiss? The Goliath birdeater (Theraphosa blondi), native to the rainforests of northern South America, has a leg span of 11 inches (28 cm) and can weigh over 6 oz (170 g) — the largest spider by mass on Earth. When threatened, it rubs specialized hairs on its legs together to produce a hissing sound audible from 15 feet (4.6 m) away, a behavior called stridulation. It also kicks clouds of barbed, irritant hairs from its abdomen into an attacker's face. Despite its name, the Goliath birdeater rarely eats birds, feeding primarily on earthworms, frogs, and large insects. (Source: Guinness World Records)

☑ Can a Spider's Fangs Puncture a Mouse Skull? The Goliath birdeater possesses fangs measuring up to 1.5 inches (3.8 cm) long — comparable in length to a cheetah's claws and large enough to pierce the skulls of small vertebrates. Unlike most spiders, which liquefy prey externally and drink the resulting fluid, the Goliath birdeater uses these oversized fangs to physically break through hard exoskeletons and bone before injecting digestive enzymes. Its venom is relatively mild to humans, roughly equivalent to a wasp sting, but its mechanical bite force is disproportionately powerful for an invertebrate. Researchers have documented it subduing prey as large as juvenile possums in its native Amazonian habitat. (Source: Journal of Arachnology, 2005)

☑ What Is the Largest Colony of Any Single Animal Species on Earth? Leafcutter ant colonies in Central and South America can house up to eight million workers in underground cities spanning more than 2,000 square feet (186 square meters) of chamber space. Excavations of abandoned colonies have revealed networks extending 26 feet (8 m) deep, containing thousands of interconnected rooms with specialized chambers for waste disposal, ventilation, and the cultivation of the fungal gardens that sustain the colony. A single mature colony moves an estimated 40 tons (36 metric tons) of soil during construction — an engineering output per capita that no other animal matches. (Source: PNAS)

☑ Which Aquatic Animal Has the Fastest Burst Acceleration of Any Swimmer? While the sailfish holds the record for top sustained swimming speed, the mako shark accelerates faster than any other fish, launching from near-stationary to 46 mph (74 km/h) in a single explosive burst. Its body is densely packed with red muscle fibers tuned for power output, and specialized blood vessel networks called retia mirabilia warm its muscles above ambient water temperature — a feature shared with tunas and great white sharks but perfected in the mako for raw acceleration. This thermal advantage gives the mako roughly 50% more muscle power at depth than a comparably sized cold-bodied fish. (Source: Journal of Experimental Biology, 2005)

☑ How Fast Must the World's Smallest Warm-Blooded Animal Eat to Stay Alive? The bee hummingbird must visit an estimated 1,500 flowers per day to fuel a metabolism that burns energy faster, relative to body weight, than any other bird. Its heart rate during flight exceeds 1,200 beats per minute, and its body temperature runs at roughly 104 degrees F (40 degrees C). Each night, the bird enters a state called torpor, dropping its metabolic rate by up to 95% and lowering its body temperature to near ambient levels to survive until morning. Without this nightly shutdown, it would exhaust its energy reserves and die before dawn. (Source: The Auk: Ornithological Advances, 2018)

☑ Which Animal Is Longer Than a Blue Whale — but Has No Brain, No Heart, and No Bones? The lion's mane jellyfish (Cyanea capillata) holds the record for the longest animal on Earth, with tentacles stretching up to 120 feet (36.5 m) — exceeding the blue whale's 100-foot (30.5 m) body length. Found primarily in the cold waters of the North Atlantic and Arctic, it trails hundreds of hair-thin tentacles behind a bell that can reach 6 feet (1.8 m) in diameter. Despite its immense reach, the entire organism is over 95% water, with no centralized brain directing its movement. (Source: Marine Biology, 2010)

☑ How Does a Shark Replace 20,000 Teeth in a Single Lifetime Without Missing a Meal? The great white shark grows its teeth on a conveyor-belt system, with new rows forming behind existing ones and rotating forward as older teeth are lost. A single shark may produce and shed over 20,000 teeth across its lifespan, replacing each one in as little as eight days. Each tooth is serrated like a steak knife and coated with fluorapatite, a crystal harder than human dental enamel. The replacement cycle never pauses — at any given moment, a great white carries several rows in various stages of development behind the functional front row. (Source: Journal of Morphology, 2012)

☑ Could a Single Aphid Theoretically Produce More Descendants in One Season Than There Are Stars in the Milky Way? Under ideal conditions with no predation, disease, or food limitation, a single aphid's exponential clonal reproduction could yield roughly 600 billion descendants within one growing season. The Milky Way contains an estimated 100 to 400 billion stars. This staggering theoretical output is possible because each female is born already carrying embryos, a phenomenon called telescoping of generations. In practice, predators, parasites, and weather reduce actual populations to a fraction of this figure, but the reproductive ceiling is unmatched. (Source: Proceedings of the Royal Society B, 2002)

☑ Is There a Fish With Four Hearts — That Sometimes Relies on Just One? The hagfish, a jawless scavenger found on ocean floors worldwide, has four separate hearts: one central branchial heart and three accessory hearts located near its head, liver, and tail. The accessory hearts are simple muscular pumps that boost blood flow through specific body regions independently. In low-oxygen conditions, the branchial heart can sustain circulation alone for up to 36 hours, while the accessory hearts shut down to conserve energy. Hagfish blood pressure is the lowest of any vertebrate, so low that gravity alone can shift blood pooling to whichever end of the body hangs lower. (Source: Journal of Experimental Biology, 1998)

☑ Why Are the Giant Squid's Eyes the Size of Dinner Plates? The giant squid (Architeuthis dux) possesses eyes measuring up to 10 inches (25 cm) in diameter — the largest of any living animal. Researchers at Duke University calculated that eyes this size are not optimized for general deep-sea vision but for detecting the faint bioluminescent trails produced by sperm whales approaching from hundreds of feet away. The enormous pupil gathers enough photons to register this dim glow in near-total darkness. No smaller eye could achieve the same detection range at the depths where squid and whale routinely encounter each other. (Source: Current Biology, 2012)

☑ Can a Male Silk Moth Detect a Single Molecule of Scent Floating in a Thousand Cubic Feet of Air? The male silk moth (Bombyx mori) responds to bombykol, a pheromone released by the female, at concentrations as low as one molecule per 1,000 cubic feet of air. Its feathery antennae contain roughly 17,000 receptor cells tuned exclusively to this one chemical. Wind-tunnel experiments showed that a male can lock onto a pheromone plume and navigate upwind to a female over distances exceeding 6 miles (10 km). No artificial sensor approaches this level of molecular sensitivity for a single target compound. (Source: Journal of Insect Physiology, 1971)

☑ Why Does an African Elephant Carry Its Calf for Nearly Two Full Years Before Giving Birth? At 22 months, the African elephant has the longest gestation period of any land mammal. The extended pregnancy allows the calf's brain to develop to a level of maturity unmatched by other newborn herbivores — an elephant calf can stand, walk, and follow the herd within hours of birth, yet its brain continues growing for years. Among all vertebrates, the frilled shark holds the longest gestation at 42 months. The elephant's marathon pregnancy reflects the enormous neural complexity required to navigate a social species' intricate family dynamics. (Source: Elephant Voices, Poole)

☑ Was the Largest Land Animal Ever Heavier Than a Fully Loaded Boeing 737? Patagotitan mayorum, a titanosaur sauropod unearthed in Patagonia, Argentina, in 2014, is among the strongest candidates for the heaviest land animal in history. Estimates based on limb bone circumference place its mass at 69 tons (63 metric tons) — roughly equal to a loaded Boeing 737. It measured approximately 120 feet (37 m) from snout to tail. The competing contender, Argentinosaurus huinculensis, may have been slightly heavier, but fewer bones survive, making its mass estimate less precise. Both lived roughly 100 million years ago in what is now southern Argentina. (Source: Proceedings of the Royal Society B, 2017)

☑ How Do Scientists Weigh an Animal That Has Been Dead for 100 Million Years? Paleontologists estimate dinosaur mass using limb bone scaling: the circumference of a weight-bearing bone — typically the femur or humerus — correlates predictably with total body mass in living animals. By measuring fossil bones and applying these equations, researchers extrapolate mass for extinct species. The method has been validated against living elephants, giraffes, and cattle with an accuracy of within 10 to 15%. For incomplete skeletons, scientists compare available bones to more complete relatives and adjust proportionally — explaining why mass estimates for the same species can differ by several tons across research teams. (Source: Journal of Vertebrate Paleontology, 2012)

☑ What Contracts 90 Times Per Second — Faster Than a Hummingbird's Wingbeat? The rattlesnake's tail-shaker muscles contract at 90 times per second, making them the fastest-contracting vertebrate muscles ever measured. For comparison, a hummingbird's flight muscles beat roughly 80 times per second. The shaker muscles achieve this rate by maintaining permanently elevated calcium levels inside the cell — bypassing the release-and-reabsorb cycle that limits speed in other muscles. Rattlesnakes can sustain this vibration for hours without fatigue, a feat no other vertebrate muscle tissue replicates. The rattle itself is made of interlocking keratin segments that amplify the vibration into the distinctive warning buzz. (Source: Journal of Experimental Biology, 2003)

☑ Does an Earthworm Have Five Hearts — or Something Even Stranger? Earthworms possess five pairs of aortic arches — muscular loops that squeeze blood forward through their closed circulatory system. These are not true hearts with chambers and valves, but they perform the same essential function: generating rhythmic contractions that push blood through vessels running the entire body length. Each pair beats independently, and if one fails, the others compensate. This decentralized design means an earthworm has no single point of cardiac failure — and the system is so efficient that oxygenated blood reaches every segment despite the worm having no lungs, relying entirely on gas exchange through moist skin. (Source: Invertebrate Zoology, Ruppert & Barnes, 2004)

☑ **What Is the Most Venomous Animal on Earth — and How Is "Most Venomous" Even Measured?** The Australian box jellyfish (Chironex fleckeri) is widely regarded as the most venomous animal alive, with enough toxin in a single specimen to kill more than 60 people. Untreated stings can cause cardiac arrest in as little as three minutes. The designation depends on distinguishing venom from poison: venom is injected through a wound; poison is ingested or absorbed. A venomous animal delivers its toxin actively. (Source: Medical Journal of Australia, 2012)

☑ **Can an Animal's Entire Genetic Code Fit Inside a Fraction of the Space a Human Genome Occupies?** The parasitic microsporidian Encephalitozoon intestinalis has one of the smallest known animal-associated genomes at roughly 2.3 million base pairs — about 1,400 times smaller than the human genome. Among free-living animals, the Antarctic midge Belgica antarctica holds the record for the smallest insect genome at 99 million base pairs. These minimal genomes shed genes for any function the organism can obtain from its host or environment, proving that genetic complexity and biological success are not the same thing. (Source: Genome Research, 2009)

☑ **Does Any Animal Carry a Genome 40 Times Larger Than a Human's — and What Does That Actually Mean?** The marbled lungfish (Protopterus aethiopicus) holds the record for the largest known animal genome at approximately 130 billion base pairs — about 40 times the size of the human genome. Yet the lungfish is not 40 times more complex than a human. Much of its genome consists of repetitive sequences and transposable elements with no known function. This discrepancy is called the C-value paradox: genome size does not correlate with organismal complexity. Some of the simplest organisms carry enormous genomes, while some of the most sophisticated carry compact ones. (Source: Nature, 2021)

☑ **How Hard Does a Saltwater Crocodile Bite — and How Does Science Measure a Force That Powerful?** The saltwater crocodile (Crocodylus porosus) has the strongest measured bite force of any living animal at 3,700 pounds per square inch (psi), recorded using force transducers fitted to metal plates placed between its jaws. For comparison, a human bite generates roughly 162 psi, and a great white shark approximately 669 psi. Despite this crushing force, the muscles that open a crocodile's jaws are so weak that a person can hold the mouth shut with bare hands. The asymmetry reflects a jaw evolved exclusively for clamping, not for the chewing motions mammals require. (Source: Journal of Zoology, 2012)

☑ Which Animal Was the First True Millipede — Discovered With 1,306 Legs in 2021? Despite their name meaning "thousand feet," no millipede had ever been found with more than 750 legs — until 2021, when Eumillipes persephone was discovered 200 feet (60 m) underground in a mining borehole in Western Australia. This eyeless, thread-like species measured just 3.7 inches (95 mm) long and bore 1,306 legs across 330 body segments. Its extreme leg count likely reflects adaptation to navigating narrow underground mineral fissures. The discovery finally delivered on the millipede name's 250-year-old promise — confirming that a thousand-legged animal does, in fact, exist. (Source: Scientific Reports, 2021)

☑ Why Does the Narwhal Grow a Tusk That Can Reach 10 Feet Long — Straight Through Its Own Lip? The narwhal's tusk is an elongated upper left canine tooth that spirals counterclockwise and erupts directly through the animal's lip, reaching up to 10 feet (3 m). It contains roughly ten million nerve endings wired to the brain, making it one of the most sensitive external organs in the mammal world. Males use tusks in sparring displays, but the organ also detects changes in water temperature, salinity, and pressure. Roughly one in 500 narwhals grows two tusks — one from each canine socket — both spiraling in the same direction. (Source: The Anatomical Record, 2014)

☑ Can a Single Fish Release 300 Million Eggs at Once — and Why Does It Need That Many? The ocean sunfish (Mola mola) produces more eggs in a single spawning event than any other known vertebrate — up to 300 million at a time. Each egg is barely one millimeter in diameter and is released into open water with no parental care. The staggering number compensates for astronomical mortality: newly hatched sunfish weigh a fraction of a gram, yet adults can exceed 5,000 pounds (2,268 kg). The growth ratio from hatchling to adult is roughly 60 million to one — the greatest size increase of any vertebrate on Earth. (Source: Journal of Fish Biology, 2010)

☑ How Does the Tallest Animal on Earth Pump Blood to a Brain 18 Feet Above Its Heart? The giraffe stands up to 19 feet (5.8 m) tall and requires the highest blood pressure of any land mammal — roughly 280/180 mmHg, about twice the human average — to push blood upward through a 6-foot (1.8 m) neck to the brain. Elastic blood vessels and one-way valves prevent catastrophic blood rushes when the head drops to drink. Without these adaptations, bending down would force blood into the brain at pressures high enough to cause fatal hemorrhaging. Engineers have applied the giraffe's valve design to anti-gravity suits worn by fighter pilots. (Source: Comparative Biochemistry and Physiology, 2009)

☑ Is There an Insect the Size of a Grain of Rice That Produces a Sound Louder Than a Passing Freight Train? The lesser water boatman (Micronecta scholtzi), a freshwater insect just 2 mm long, produces mating calls measured at 99 decibels — equivalent to standing near a passing freight train. It generates this sound by rubbing a ridged appendage against its abdomen in a process called stridulation, performed entirely underwater. Relative to body size, it is the loudest animal on Earth. Most of the sound is lost at the air-water boundary, sparing human eardrums, but hydrophone recordings confirmed this single insect creates noise intensity exceeding that of far larger animals. (Source: PLOS ONE, 2011)

Venom, Poison, and Chemical Warfare

☑ What Is the Difference Between a Venomous Animal and a Poisonous One? Venom must be injected through a wound — via a fang, stinger, or spine — while poison must be ingested, inhaled, or absorbed through the skin. A rattlesnake is venomous because it delivers toxins through hollow fangs. A poison dart frog is poisonous because its skin secretes compounds that harm anything touching or eating it. The distinction matters medically: venomous bites require pressure immobilization or antivenom, while poisoning demands decontamination or activated charcoal. Confusing the two can mean applying the wrong treatment entirely. (Source: Clinical Toxicology, 2008)

☑ How Toxic Is the World's Most Venomous Snake — Drop for Drop? The inland taipan of central Australia delivers approximately 44 mg of venom in a single bite — enough to kill over 100 adult humans. Its LD50 — the dose lethal to half the test subjects — is 0.025 mg per kilogram, making it roughly 50 times more potent than the Indian cobra. Despite this extraordinary toxicity, human fatalities are virtually unheard of because the inland taipan inhabits remote semi-arid plains and is extremely reclusive. Every confirmed bite on record has been treated successfully with antivenom. (Source: Australian Venom Research Unit, 2001)

☑ **How Does Box Jellyfish Venom Kill a Healthy Adult in Three Minutes?** The Australian box jellyfish (Chironex fleckeri) injects venom through billions of microscopic nematocysts lining its tentacles. The toxin attacks cardiac muscle cells directly, punching holes in their membranes and flooding them with calcium ions. The heart muscle contracts uncontrollably, then stops. Untreated stings can cause cardiac arrest in as little as three minutes. A single adult specimen carries enough venom to kill more than 60 people — yet the jellyfish has no brain, no blood, and no centralized nervous system directing the attack. (Source: Medical Journal of Australia, 2012)

☑ **What Is the Fastest Biological Mechanism Ever Measured — and It Belongs to a Jellyfish?** A cnidarian nematocyst fires in approximately 700 nanoseconds — less than one millionth of a second — generating an acceleration exceeding 5 million times the force of gravity. The coiled harpoon-like thread pierces prey tissue faster than any other known biological action. Each tentacle of a box jellyfish carries millions of these capsules, primed under enormous internal pressure, and no muscle contraction triggers the discharge — mechanical and chemical contact alone cause instantaneous release. (Source: Current Biology, 2006)

☑ **Can a Slow-Moving Sea Snail Really Kill a Fish With a Single Venomous Strike?** Cone snails fire a hollow, barbed radula tooth like a hypodermic harpoon into passing fish. The tooth injects a cocktail of 100 to 200 distinct peptide toxins called conotoxins, each targeting a different ion channel or receptor in the nervous system. The combined effect paralyzes the fish within seconds. Because each conotoxin locks onto one molecular target with extreme precision, pharmaceutical researchers have identified cone snail peptides as templates for drugs treating chronic pain, epilepsy, and cardiovascular disease. (Source: Nature Reviews Drug Discovery, 2004)

☑ **Why Is the Blue-Ringed Octopus Deadly Despite Being Smaller Than a Human Hand?** The blue-ringed octopus carries tetrodotoxin — a neurotoxin 1,000 times more toxic than cyanide — produced not by the octopus itself but by symbiotic bacteria living in its salivary glands. TTX blocks sodium channels in nerve cells, shutting down signal transmission between the brain and muscles. Victims remain fully conscious as respiratory paralysis sets in. No antidote exists; survival depends entirely on artificial ventilation until the toxin clears. The octopus itself is immune because its sodium channels carry a genetic mutation that prevents TTX from binding. (Source: PLOS ONE, 2011)

☑ Is It True That Platypus Venom Causes Pain So Severe That Morphine Cannot Relieve It? Male platypuses deliver venom through sharp spurs on their hind ankles — one of the few venomous mammals on Earth. The venom contains defensin-like peptides that activate pain receptors through a mechanism entirely different from snake venom. Victims describe the agony as immediate, incapacitating, and resistant to standard opioid painkillers, including morphine. The spur is used primarily during mating-season competition between males. Researchers studying platypus venom have identified novel pain pathways that may eventually help develop new analgesics for human patients with treatment-resistant chronic pain. (Source: Journal of Investigative Dermatology, 2010)

☑ Why Are Poison Dart Frogs Harmless in Captivity but Lethal in the Wild? The golden poison frog (Phyllobates terribilis) carries enough batrachotoxin on its skin to kill ten adult humans — yet captive-bred individuals are completely non-toxic. The poison is not self-produced. Wild frogs sequester alkaloid toxins from the beetles, ants, and mites they consume in their native Colombian rainforest. Remove the dietary source, and toxicity vanishes within months. Indigenous Emberá people harvest wild frogs' skin secretions to coat blowgun darts — a practice that gave the entire family its common name. (Source: PNAS, 2004)

☑ **How Many Times Has Evolution Independently Invented Venom?** Venom has evolved independently in more than 100 animal lineages — across snakes, spiders, jellyfish, insects, fish, mammals, and even some crustaceans. Molecular analysis reveals that many unrelated venomous species repurposed the same ancestral genes: harmless salivary proteins, digestive enzymes, and immune-system molecules were duplicated and modified into toxins through convergent evolution. The phenomenon suggests that the genetic raw material for venom production is widespread in animal genomes, and natural selection has found the same biochemical solution repeatedly across hundreds of millions of years. (Source: Annual Review of Genomics and Human Genetics, 2009)

☑ **Did Three Entirely Different Snake Fang Designs Really Evolve Independently to Solve the Same Problem?** Venomous snakes deliver venom through three distinct fang architectures that evolved independently. Vipers possess solenoglyphous fangs — long, hollow, hinged needles that fold against the palate when the mouth closes. Cobras and mambas have proteroglyphous fangs — short, fixed, front-mounted tubes. Rear-fanged colubrids use opisthoglyphous fangs — grooved teeth at the back of the jaw that channel venom by capillary action. Each system injects toxin effectively, yet none shares an evolutionary blueprint with the others. (Source: Journal of Morphology, 2008)

☑ Can a Black Mamba's Bite Kill a Human in Under an Hour? The black mamba (Dendroaspis polylepis) injects a potent cocktail of dendrotoxins that block potassium channels in nerve cells, causing rapid neuromuscular paralysis. A single bite delivers enough venom to kill 15 adults. Without antivenom, respiratory failure can occur within 45 minutes. The mamba compounds this danger with speed — it is the fastest snake on Earth, capable of short bursts exceeding 12 mph (19 km/h) — and will deliver multiple bites in rapid succession when cornered rather than fleeing. (Source: Toxicon, 2011)

☑ Why Does a Puff Adder's Bite Destroy Tissue Instead of Shutting Down Nerves? Unlike neurotoxic mamba venom, the puff adder (Bitis arietans) produces primarily cytotoxic venom — enzymes that digest cell membranes, blood vessel walls, and muscle tissue around the bite site. The result is massive localized swelling, tissue necrosis, and hemorrhage that can lead to permanent disfigurement or limb amputation even when the patient survives. Cytotoxic venoms evolved to serve a dual purpose: immobilizing prey and beginning external digestion before the snake has even swallowed its meal. (Source: Toxicology Letters, 2009)

☑ Did You Know That Horses Are the Unlikely Heroes Behind Almost Every Antivenom on Earth? Producing antivenom requires injecting a large animal with gradually increasing doses of diluted venom over several months. The animal's immune system generates antibodies, which are then extracted from its blood and purified. Horses are preferred because their large blood volume yields commercially viable quantities of antibodies per cycle. The process has remained essentially unchanged since Albert Calmette developed the first antivenom against cobra venom in 1895, and no synthetic alternative has yet matched its effectiveness at scale. (Source: World Health Organization, 2010)

☑ Do Venomous Snakebites Kill More People Each Year Than Landmines and Cluster Bombs Combined? The World Health Organization estimates that venomous snakebites kill between 81,000 and 138,000 people annually, with up to 400,000 more suffering permanent disability. Sub-Saharan Africa and South Asia bear the highest burden. Despite these figures, antivenom production has declined because manufacturers cannot profit from selling to impoverished rural populations. Several critical African antivenoms were discontinued in the 2010s, leaving entire regions with no locally effective treatment available at any price. (Source: World Health Organization, 2019)

☑ **Which Blood Pressure Pill Taken by Millions Was Designed by Copying a Pit Viper's Venom?** In the 1960s, Brazilian pharmacologist Sérgio Ferreira discovered that venom from the lancehead pit viper (Bothrops jararaca) contained a peptide that dramatically lowered blood pressure by inhibiting angiotensin-converting enzyme. That peptide became the template for captopril — the first ACE inhibitor — approved in 1981 and now one of the most widely prescribed cardiovascular drug classes on Earth. A molecule evolved to incapacitate prey became the foundation for medicines that have saved millions of human lives. (Source: Hypertension, 2003)

☑ **How Did a Cone Snail's Toxin Become a Painkiller Stronger Than Morphine?** Ziconotide, derived from the omega-conotoxin of the marine cone snail Conus magus, blocks N-type calcium channels in spinal nerve cells with extraordinary specificity. Approved by the FDA in 2004, it is delivered directly into the spinal fluid for patients with severe chronic pain who no longer respond to opioids. Unlike morphine, ziconotide carries no risk of addiction or respiratory depression. A single peptide from a slow-moving predatory snail now offers relief where the most powerful conventional painkillers have failed. (Source: Journal of Pain Research, 2006)

☑ **What Does It Feel Like to Be Stung by the Insect That Tops the Pain Scale?** Entomologist Justin O. Schmidt deliberately allowed himself to be stung by dozens of Hymenoptera species and rated the pain on a four-point index. The bullet ant (Paraponera clavata) of Central and South American rainforests earned the maximum rating of 4.0+ — described as waves of burning, throbbing agony lasting up to 24 hours without diminishing. The Sáteré-Mawé people of Brazil use intentional bullet ant stings as an initiation rite, requiring young men to wear gloves filled with the ants for ten minutes. (Source: Schmidt, 1990)

☑ Which Wasp Delivers the Second Most Painful Sting on Earth — and Uses It to Paralyze a Spider Alive? The tarantula hawk wasp (Pepsis grossa) scores 4.0 on Schmidt's sting pain index — level with the bullet ant. Schmidt described the sensation as a blinding, electric shock that shuts down all rational thought for approximately three minutes. The wasp uses its sting not in defense but to paralyze tarantulas many times its own weight. The paralyzed spider, still alive, is dragged into a burrow where the wasp lays a single egg on its abdomen. The hatching larva then consumes the spider from the inside out. (Source: Annals of the Entomological Society of America, 2016)

☑ Can a Jellyfish the Size of a Fingernail Cause a Feeling of Impending Death? Irukandji syndrome is triggered by stings from Carukia barnesi and related jellyfish measuring barely 0.4 inches (1 cm) across — so small they pass through standard safety nets. Thirty minutes after an almost painless sting, victims experience severe back pain, nausea, and a documented psychological symptom unique in medicine: an overwhelming, specific sense of impending doom so intense that patients beg doctors to let them die. The syndrome can cause brain hemorrhage and heart failure. No antivenom exists. (Source: Medical Journal of Australia, 2002)

☑ Why Do Some of the Deadliest Sea Snakes Rarely Kill Humans Despite Having Venom More Toxic Than a Cobra's? The Dubois' sea snake (Aipysurus duboisii) and the beaked sea snake possess venom more potent than any terrestrial cobra, yet human fatalities are rare. Sea snakes have small fangs, inject minimal venom per bite, and are generally reluctant to bite at all. Their venom evolved to immobilize fast-moving fish underwater — a task requiring extreme potency in tiny doses because venom disperses rapidly in seawater. The mismatch between lethal potential and actual danger illustrates how venom potency reflects ecological need, not aggression. (Source: Toxicon, 2015)

☑ How Did a Venomous Lizard From the Arizona Desert Become the Basis for a Blockbuster Diabetes Drug? The Gila monster (Heloderma suspectum) produces exendin-4, a peptide in its venom that mimics a human gut hormone called GLP-1 but resists enzymatic breakdown far longer than the natural version. Pharmaceutical researchers synthesized a near-identical molecule called exenatide, marketed as Byetta, and approved for Type 2 diabetes in 2005. It stimulates insulin release only when blood sugar is elevated, reducing the risk of dangerous hypoglycemia. A venom component evolved to disrupt prey metabolism now regulates blood sugar in millions of patients worldwide. (Source: Journal of Biological Chemistry, 2005)

☑ Which Mammal Paralyzes Its Prey With Venomous Saliva and Stores Them Alive in Underground Larders? The northern short-tailed shrew (Blarina brevicauda) is one of the few venomous mammals on Earth. Its submaxillary glands secrete a kallikrein-like protease called blarina toxin, delivered through grooved lower incisors. The venom lowers blood pressure and induces paralysis in earthworms, snails, and small rodents without killing them outright. The shrew then drags immobilized prey into underground caches where they remain alive but unable to move — a living food supply preserved fresh for days. This strategy evolved because shrews must consume nearly their own body weight in food every 24 hours to survive. (Source: Journal of Mammalogy, 2004)

☑ Can a Caterpillar's Sting Cause Fatal Hemorrhaging Throughout the Entire Human Body? The South American caterpillar Lonomia obliqua — the "assassin caterpillar" — carries hollow, venom-filled spines that release a potent anticoagulant and fibrinolytic cocktail on contact. Victims who brush against a cluster on a tree trunk may develop disseminated intravascular coagulation — uncontrolled bleeding from the gums, kidneys, and brain. Between 1989 and 2005, over 500 confirmed envenomation cases were recorded in southern Brazil, with a fatality rate approaching 2.5%. An antivenom developed by the Butantan Institute in São Paulo remains the only effective treatment. (Source: Toxicon, 2006)

☑ Why Does Black Widow Venom Devastate Insects but Rarely Kill Humans? The western black widow (Latrodectus hesperus) produces alpha-latrotoxin, which forces massive, uncontrolled neurotransmitter release at nerve-muscle junctions. In insects, whose small body mass concentrates the toxin rapidly, the effect is fatal within seconds. In humans, the same mechanism causes intense muscle cramping, abdominal pain, and elevated blood pressure — a condition called latrodectism — but the toxin distributes across a body mass roughly 40,000 times greater than the spider's typical prey. Fewer than 1% of untreated bites result in death, and fatalities in healthy adults are exceptionally rare. (Source: New England Journal of Medicine, 2014)

☑ Why Is the World's Most Venomous Fish Almost Impossible to See Before You Step on It? The reef stonefish (Synanceia verrucosa) lies motionless on the seafloor, its mottled, warty skin indistinguishable from the surrounding rock and coral. Thirteen dorsal spines each contain a venom gland that discharges under mechanical pressure, typically a human foot. The venom produces immediate, excruciating pain described by victims as the worst they have ever experienced, followed by rapid tissue necrosis, cardiovascular collapse, and potential limb loss. Wading without protective footwear in Indo-Pacific reef shallows remains the primary mechanism of human envenomation. (Source: Toxicon, 2013)

☑ Can a Rattlesnake Choose How Much Venom to Inject — or Choose Not to Inject Any at All? Rattlesnakes meter their venom delivery with remarkable precision. Studies show that between 25% and 50% of defensive bites on humans are "dry bites" — strikes that inject no venom. When venom is deployed, the quantity varies depending on the perceived threat level and whether the strike is defensive or predatory. Venom production is metabolically expensive: regenerating a full supply after complete discharge requires up to three weeks, during which the snake hunts less effectively. Metering venom conserves a limited and costly resource that the snake cannot afford to waste on every encounter. (Source: Toxicon, 2002)

☑ What Makes the King Cobra Unique Among All Venomous Snakes? The king cobra (Ophiophagus hannah) is the longest venomous snake on Earth, reaching up to 18 feet (5.5 m). Its Latin name means "snake eater" — and its diet consists almost entirely of other snakes, including venomous species. A single bite delivers up to 7 ml of venom, enough to kill an adult elephant. Unlike most cobra venoms, which rely primarily on postsynaptic neurotoxins, king cobra venom contains a unique cytotoxin called ohanin that causes pain, lethargy, and hypothermia in prey — a compound found in no other snake species studied to date. (Source: Nature, 2013)

☑ How Does a Monarch Butterfly Become Toxic Without Producing Any Poison Itself? Monarch caterpillars feed exclusively on milkweed plants, which contain cardenolides — cardiac glycosides that disrupt sodium-potassium pumps in heart muscle. The caterpillar sequesters these toxins in its tissues, retaining them through metamorphosis into adulthood. A bird that eats a monarch experiences violent vomiting within minutes. Most predators learn to associate the butterfly's vivid orange-and-black pattern with this consequence and avoid monarchs permanently after a single encounter. The butterfly pays no metabolic cost for its defense — the milkweed plant manufactures the weapon, and the monarch simply borrows it. (Source: PNAS, 1968)

☑ How Does an Ant Smaller Than a Pencil Eraser Inflict Pain That Lasts for Hours? The red imported fire ant (Solenopsis invicta) stings by anchoring its mandibles into skin and pivoting its abdomen to inject venom from a modified ovipositor. The venom is 95% solenopsin — a unique piperidine alkaloid that destroys cell membranes on contact, producing the characteristic burning pain and sterile pustules that appear within 24 hours. A single fire ant colony can contain over 200,000 workers, and coordinated mass stinging events have caused anaphylaxis and, in rare cases, death. Since arriving in Alabama around 1930, fire ants have spread across the southeastern United States. (Source: Annual Review of Entomology, 2005)

☑ Which Common Backyard Animal Is Immune to Rattlesnake Venom — and How Did It Evolve That Defense? The Virginia opossum (Didelphis virginiana) carries a peptide in its blood serum called lethal toxin-neutralizing factor, which binds to and neutralizes rattlesnake venom proteins on contact. The opossum can survive bites from pit vipers that would kill a similarly sized mammal within hours. Researchers at San José State University demonstrated that the synthetic version of this peptide protects mice from otherwise lethal doses of venom — raising the possibility of a cheap, shelf-stable universal antivenom based on an opossum's blood chemistry. (Source: Journal of Venomous Animals and Toxins, 2015)

☑ Is the Slow Loris Really the Only Primate That Produces and Deploys Venom? The slow loris (Nycticebus spp.) secretes a toxin from brachial glands on its inner elbows. When threatened, it licks these glands and mixes the secretion with saliva, creating a compound that causes severe allergic reactions, tissue necrosis, and anaphylactic shock in some bite victims. The toxin's chemistry closely resembles the allergenic protein Fel d 1 found in domestic cat dander — suggesting an evolutionary link between primate venom and mammalian allergen pathways. The slow loris also anoints its fur and offspring with the toxin, creating a chemical shield against parasites and predators. (Source: Journal of Venomous Animals and Toxins, 2013)

☑ Which Giant Centipede Produces a Toxin That Blocks Pain More Selectively Than Morphine? The Chinese red-headed centipede (Scolopendra subspinipes mutilans) produces a peptide toxin called SsTx that blocks the Nav1.7 sodium channel — a receptor directly linked to human pain perception. Unlike morphine, SsTx does not cross-react with opioid receptors and carries no risk of addiction or respiratory depression. In laboratory trials, the peptide blocked inflammatory and chemical pain in mice as effectively as morphine at equivalent doses. Humans with natural Nav1.7 mutations feel no pain at all, confirming this channel as one of the most promising targets for next-generation analgesics derived from animal venom. (Source: PNAS, 2013)

☑ Is Scorpion Venom the Most Expensive Liquid on Earth — and Why Does It Cost More Than Gold? Deathstalker scorpion (Leiurus quinquestriatus) venom is valued at approximately $39 million per gallon because each scorpion yields only about two milligrams per extraction, and the process requires manual stimulation of the venom glands. The cost reflects both scarcity and pharmaceutical demand: a peptide in the venom called chlorotoxin binds selectively to glioma cells — a type of aggressive brain cancer — without attaching to healthy tissue. Surgeons now use fluorescent-labeled chlorotoxin to illuminate tumor margins during brain surgery, distinguishing cancerous tissue from healthy brain in real time. (Source: Cancer Research, 2007)

☑ Which Snake Kills More Humans Annually Than Any Other Species on Earth? The saw-scaled viper (Echis carinatus) is responsible for more human snakebite deaths than any other single species. Found across the Indian subcontinent, the Middle East, and parts of Africa, it favors agricultural land and human settlements. It is small — rarely exceeding 2 feet (60 cm) — highly aggressive when disturbed, and often encountered by barefoot farmworkers at dusk. Its hemotoxic venom causes uncontrolled internal bleeding and kidney failure. Unlike reclusive species with higher venom potency, the saw-scaled viper's lethality comes from proximity to dense human populations, nocturnal activity, and an exceptionally low threshold for defensive striking. (Source: The Lancet, 2010)

☑ Which Spider's Bite Can Trigger a Four-Hour Erection as a Medical Side Effect? The Brazilian wandering spider (Phoneutria nigriventer), one of the most venomous arachnids on Earth, produces a neurotoxin called PhTx3 that causes intense pain, salivation, and irregular heartbeat. In male victims, one component — the peptide PnTx2-6 — triggers prolonged, painful priapism by increasing nitric oxide release in erectile tissue. Researchers at the Medical College of Georgia found that a modified version of this peptide restores erectile function in animal models of impotence without the dangerous side effects of the raw venom. A spider bite's most notorious symptom may lead to treatments for erectile dysfunction. (Source: Journal of Sexual Medicine, 2012)

☑ Can Honeybee Venom Destroy Cancer Cells While Leaving Healthy Cells Intact? Melittin, the primary active component of European honeybee (Apis mellifera) venom, punches holes in cell membranes by integrating into their lipid bilayers. Research at the Harry Perkins Institute demonstrated that synthetic melittin killed triple-negative breast cancer cells and HER2-enriched cancer cells within 60 minutes while causing minimal damage to normal cells at the same concentration. The mechanism disrupts cancer cell signaling pathways that drive replication. Melittin has also shown anti-tumor activity against melanoma and lung cancer cells in preclinical studies, positioning bee venom as a platform for targeted cancer therapies. (Source: Nature Precision Oncology, 2020)

☑ Why Do Millipedes Smell Like Almonds — and Why Should That Worry You? Many millipede species, particularly those in the order Polydesmida, produce hydrogen cyanide gas from glands along their body segments when disturbed. The almond-like odor is the same compound used in industrial poisons. A single large tropical millipede can release enough HCN to kill a mouse in a sealed container. This chemical defense is not venom — it requires no injection mechanism — but functions as a contact-and-inhalation deterrent. Some species supplement cyanide with quinones and phenols, creating a multi-compound chemical cocktail that irritates predator skin and mucous membranes simultaneously. (Source: Journal of Chemical Ecology, 2005)

☑ Which Arachnid Sprays Pure Vinegar at Predators From a Turret Mounted on Its Abdomen? The giant whip scorpion (Mastigoproctus giganteus), also called the vinegaroon, defends itself by spraying a concentrated solution of approximately 85% acetic acid — essentially pure vinegar — from glands at the base of its tail. The spray is aimed with remarkable accuracy at up to 19 inches (48 cm), targeting the predator's eyes and mouthparts. Despite its fearsome appearance and potent chemical defense, the vinegaroon possesses no venom glands and cannot sting. It is one of the clearest examples of an animal that relies entirely on chemical warfare without any venomous capability whatsoever. (Source: Journal of Arachnology, 2015)

☑ Why Do Non-Venomous Scarlet Kingsnakes Look Almost Identical to Deadly Coral Snakes? The scarlet kingsnake (Lampropeltis elapsoides) mimics the red, yellow, and black banding pattern of the eastern coral snake — one of North America's most venomous species. Predators that have survived or witnessed a coral snake encounter avoid anything displaying the same color sequence. The kingsnake exploits this learned avoidance without producing any venom. Studies found that kingsnake populations living closer to coral snake territory display more accurate mimicry than those living farther away, demonstrating that natural selection sharpens the disguise in proportion to the model's local presence. (Source: Proceedings of the National Academy of Sciences, 2014)

☑ How Many Venoms Remain Completely Unstudied — and What Medicines Might They Contain? Of the estimated 220,000 venomous animal species on Earth, fewer than 1% have had their venom biochemically characterized. Cone snails alone produce an estimated 200,000 distinct peptide compounds across all species, yet only a handful have been tested for pharmaceutical potential. The emerging field of venomics uses high-throughput mass spectrometry and genomic sequencing to catalog entire venom libraries simultaneously. Researchers at the University of Queensland estimate that animal venoms may contain over 20 million bioactive compounds — a virtually untapped pharmaceutical library that dwarfs any synthetic drug-screening collection assembled to date. (Source: Nature Reviews Drug Discovery, 2015)

Mysteries and Misconceptions

☑ Has Any Ostrich Ever Been Documented Burying Its Head in the Sand? No ostrich has ever been documented performing this behavior. The probable source is nest care: ostriches periodically lower their heads into a shallow ground depression to turn eggs with their beaks, which, from a distance, resembles burial. Ostriches also press their heads flat to the ground as a concealment posture when they cannot flee, reducing their profile against the open savanna. The myth appears in written form in Pliny the Elder's Natural History from the first century CE, where he states that ostriches believe themselves fully hidden once their head is out of sight. That single misinterpretation has outlasted 2,000 years of formal zoology without a documented case to support it. (Source: Pliny the Elder, Naturalis Historia, 77 CE; Zoological Society of London, 2005)

☑ Did a Disney Film Crew Manufacture the Most Famous Animal Myth in Modern History? The widespread belief that lemmings commit mass suicide by hurling themselves off cliffs traces directly to the 1958 Disney documentary White Wilderness, in which a lemming stampede was staged. Filmmakers purchased animals from children in Alberta, placed them on a snow-covered turntable to simulate a running horde, then herded them off a riverbank into the water below. Wild Norwegian lemmings do experience dramatic population cycles every three to four years, driven by predation pressure and food depletion, and dispersing animals sometimes drown crossing rivers — but mass intentional cliff-jumping has never once been documented in nature. (Source: Canadian Broadcasting Corporation, 1982)

☑ Does Science Actually Confirm That a Goldfish Has Only a Three-Second Memory? No peer-reviewed research supports this claim, and multiple controlled experiments have directly contradicted it. In 2003, researchers at Plymouth University trained goldfish to press a lever for food at specific times of day — a task requiring the animal to track time across several weeks. A separate conditioning study demonstrated aversion memory persisting for over three months. The origin of the three-second figure is untraceable to any published scientific paper. Goldfish are neurologically capable of associative learning, time discrimination, and spatial navigation, none of which is possible without functional memory extending well beyond three seconds. (Source: University of Plymouth, 2003)

☑ What Actually Makes a Bull Charge at a Matador's Red Cape? Cattle are dichromats — they possess two types of color-receptor cone cells and cannot distinguish red from green or yellow. The specific color of the matador's cape is functionally invisible to a bull as a distinct stimulus. What triggers the charge is motion: the sweeping movement of the fabric, combined with the accumulated stress of noise, crowding, and confinement in the arena long before the cape appears. Spanish fighting bulls are selectively bred for aggression and would charge the cape regardless of its color. The traditional muleta is red, not to enrage the animal but to conceal blood from the spectators watching. (Source: Journal of Comparative Psychology, 2007)

☑ Why Did One 1947 Zoo Study Permanently Poison How Millions of People Train Their Dogs? The term "alpha wolf" originated in a 1947 paper by Swiss animal behaviorist Rudolf Schenkel, based entirely on observations of captive zoo wolves — unrelated adults forced together under artificial confinement, producing dominance contests that no field study of wild wolves has ever replicated. The dog training industry adopted the concept wholesale, generating decades of dominance-based "pack leader" methods. Controlled research published between 2004 and 2009 found that these techniques measurably increase fear, anxiety, and aggression in domestic dogs compared to reward-based approaches. A theory that caused measurable behavioral harm was built on a single study that never left a zoo enclosure. (Source: Applied Animal Behavior Science, 2009)

☑ Can a Chameleon Actually Change Its Color to Match Any Background? Chameleons do not change color primarily for camouflage, and they cannot match any arbitrary surface on demand. Their color is controlled by layers of iridophore cells containing nanocrystals that shift their spacing when the cells expand or contract, altering the wavelengths of reflected light across a limited biological palette. Males display their most vivid and varied colors during territorial confrontations and courtship — contexts requiring conspicuousness, not concealment. Temperature regulation also drives color change independently of any social signal. Background-matching camouflage occurs in some species under some conditions, but is one minor output of a system built primarily for communication and thermoregulation. (Source: Nature Communications, 2015)

☑ Does Science Actually Confirm That Elephants Never Forget? The popular saying understates the documented reality. African elephants possess a proportionally large hippocampus — the brain region central to long-term memory — even relative to their considerable overall brain mass. Field research at Amboseli documented female elephants responding with recognition calls to the playback of family members they had not heard for over ten years. A 2001 study confirmed that matriarchs can distinguish the voices of at least 100 individuals from memory alone. When presented with recordings of deceased herd members, living elephants showed prolonged, distressed investigation responses consistent with recognizing a voice that should no longer exist. Their long-term memory is among the most rigorously documented of any non-human animal. (Source: Proceedings of the Royal Society B, 2001)

☑ Are Daddy Longlegs Really the World's Most Venomous Spider, Simply Unable to Pierce Human Skin? This claim fails on two independent counts. The name "daddy longlegs" refers to at least three entirely unrelated animals. Harvestmen, in the order Opiliones, are the animals most commonly called by this name in North America: they are not spiders and produce no venom whatsoever, possessing no venom glands at all. Crane flies, called daddy longlegs across Britain, are harmless insects with no bite and no toxin. The cellar spider (Pholcus phalangioides) is the only true spider sharing the name, and controlled toxicological testing at the University of California, Riverside confirmed its venom to be of low potency — not the world's most dangerous by any tested measure. (Source: University of California, Riverside, 2004)

☑ Can Animals Commit Suicide — or Does the Concept Simply Not Apply to Non-Human Minds? Suicide requires understanding death as a future outcome and intending to cause it — a threshold no non-human animal has been confirmed to cross. Apparent animal self-destruction consistently has biological explanations. Stranded whales are typically already dying from disease or organ failure before they beach. Zombie ant fungus (Ophiocordyceps unilateralis) forces workers to die in positions ideal for spore dispersal; the ant exercises no choice. Octopus females stop eating after laying eggs and die of starvation — a genetically fixed reproductive strategy, not despair. Observable self-damaging behavior in animals is real and well-documented; intentional self-destruction, requiring comprehension of death as a concept, has not been demonstrated in any non-human species. (Source: Biological Reviews, 2018)

☑ Did the World's First Scientist to Examine a Platypus Reach for His Scissors to Check for Stitching? When the first dried platypus skin arrived in Britain in 1799, naturalist George Shaw examined it with scissors, probing for evidence that a duck bill had been sewn onto a mammal's body by a skilled taxidermist. The animal was genuine, but nothing in existing natural history had prepared European science for an egg-laying, fur-covered creature with a bill capable of detecting electrical fields and — in males — venomous ankle spurs. Shaw published his formal description with a footnote explicitly acknowledging his suspicion of fraud before accepting the animal as real. The platypus demanded that every rule of mammalian classification be rewritten around it rather than the other way around. (Source: Shaw, G., Naturalist's Miscellany, 1799)

☑ How Did a Horse-Sized Relative of the Giraffe Remain Unknown to Western Science Until 1901? The okapi (Okapia johnstoni) stands nearly five feet (1.5 m) at the shoulder, has a blue-black prehensile tongue measuring over 12 inches (30 cm), and is the only living relative of the giraffe. It inhabits the dense Ituri rainforest of what is now the Democratic Republic of Congo. Explorer Henry Stanley reported a "forest donkey" based on local accounts in the 1880s; the reports were dismissed as exaggeration. In 1901, the Natural History Museum in London formally identified the species from a specimen obtained through British colonial contacts. The okapi's discovery shifted scientific thinking permanently about what large, bodily distinct species might still exist in poorly mapped tropical habitats. (Source: Natural History Museum, London, 1901)

☑ Why Did It Take Until 2004 to Photograph a Giant Squid Alive — and Why Did a Fishing Line Succeed Where Submarines Failed? Despite decades of expeditions deploying submersibles and deep-sea camera systems, the first photographs of a living giant squid (Architeuthis dux) were taken in 2004 by Japanese researchers Tsunemi Kubodera and Kyoichi Mori using a baited drop line rigged with a remote camera at 3,000 feet (915 m) depth near Japan's Ogasawara Islands. A squid estimated at 26 feet (8 m) attacked the bait and became temporarily snagged, yielding 556 photographs over four hours before it broke free. The species had been known from carcasses and whale-skin sucker scars for over a century. The technological breakthrough came not from expensive equipment but from a hook, a camera, and patience. (Source: Proceedings of the Royal Society B, 2004)

☑ How Did a Fish Assumed Extinct for 66 Million Years Appear in a Fisherman's Net on the South African Coast? On December 22, 1938, museum curator Marjorie Courtenay-Latimer was examining a trawler's catch when she spotted a large blue fish with peculiar lobed fins she could not identify. Ichthyologist J.L.B. Smith confirmed it as a coelacanth — a lineage known only from fossils dated to 66 million BCE, assumed extinct with the non-avian dinosaurs. A second population was confirmed near the Comoros Islands in 1952, and a distinct second species, Latimeria menadoensis, was identified in Indonesian waters in 1997. A fish whose lineage science declared extinct for 66 million years had been living at depths below 490 feet (150 m), undiscovered throughout recorded human history. (Source: Nature, 1939)

☑ Are Bats Actually Blind — and If Not, Why Does Everyone Believe They Are? All bat species can see. Smaller insectivorous bats have compact eyes suited to low-light conditions and rely heavily on echolocation for prey detection, but their visual systems are functional. Large fruit bats — the flying foxes — have well-developed eyes and navigate partly by sight and smell, using echolocation far less. A 2009 study confirmed that bats actively switch between echolocation and vision depending on conditions, using visual input to update their spatial maps in real time. The phrase "blind as a bat" almost certainly originates from the animal's preference for darkness and its apparently erratic nocturnal flight — not from any documented failure of the visual system. (Source: PLOS ONE, 2009)

☑ Are Elephants Really Terrified of Mice? No peer-reviewed research documents a genuine fear response in elephants toward mice. The belief appears in ancient texts, including Pliny the Elder, and was embedded in popular culture through cartoons. In controlled observations at wildlife sanctuaries, elephants show no detectable stress response to mice placed in proximity. Their documented fears are more specific: unfamiliar sounds, fast-moving insects near the sensitive skin around their eyes, and the buzzing of African bees. A 2016 study confirmed African elephants reliably flee from playback of bee sounds — a rational response to a genuine physical threat. Mice, by contrast, produce no comparable reaction under any documented test condition. (Source: Current Biology, 2016)

☑ Is It True That a Duck's Quack Produces No Echo? This claim was formally tested by acoustics researcher Trevor Cox at the University of Salford in 2003, who recorded a duck named Daisy in both anechoic and reverberant environments. Echoes were measurable in both. The myth likely persists because duck quacks fade gradually rather than stopping abruptly, making it difficult to separate the returned echo from the tail of the original call in outdoor settings. The quack produces a perfectly normal echo — it is simply softer than most sounds at its trailing end, and the echo is softer still. Cox concluded the myth arose from natural acoustic conditions rather than any genuine property of duck vocalizations. (Source: University of Salford, Acoustics Research Center, 2003)

☑ How Did Scientists Discover a Large, Previously Unknown Mammal in Asia as Recently as 1992? The saola (Pseudoryx nghetinhensis) — a bovine roughly the size of a large deer, with two long parallel straight horns and distinctive white facial markings — was entirely unknown to science until 1992, when WWF biologists found skulls and skins in a Vietnamese hunter's home in the Annamite Mountains. No researcher has ever photographed a living individual in the field; all confirmed evidence comes from camera traps, and the last captive specimen died in 1996. Its discovery proved that morphologically distinct, large mammals can remain unknown in geographically accessible mountain ranges as recently as the final decade of the 20th century, driving intensified survey work across under-documented tropical forests worldwide. (Source: Nature, 1992)

☑ How Did a Shark Measuring 14 Feet Long Evade Scientific Detection Until 1976? The megamouth shark (Megachasma pelagios) was discovered accidentally on November 15, 1976, when a U.S. Navy vessel near Hawaii hauled up a 14.5-foot (4.4 m) specimen entangled in its sea anchor at 500 feet (150 m) depth. A deep-water filter feeder with distinctive luminescent lips and a cavernous gaping mouth, it represented an entirely new shark family — the first such family new to science in over a century. Fewer than 270 confirmed encounters had been recorded worldwide by 2023. A shark exceeding the average length of a great white had spent its entire evolutionary history in the world's oceans without leaving a single trace in the scientific record. (Source: Proceedings of the California Academy of Sciences, 1983)

☑ When an Opossum "Plays Dead," Is It Actually Choosing to Do So? The Virginia opossum (Didelphis virginiana) enters what biologists call thanatosis when threatened, but not by conscious choice. The behavior is an involuntary physiological collapse triggered by extreme fear: the animal loses muscle control, goes limp, and can remain immobile for minutes to hours, with slowed heart rate, reduced breathing, and odors consistent with decomposition. It cannot end the state by deciding to move; the response terminates only when the stimulus subsides. Many predators preferentially pursue living prey and ignore motionless animals, making involuntary death-feigning an effective last-resort defense. The opossum plays dead in the same sense that a human faints: through biological reflex, not performance. (Source: Behavioral Processes, 2012)

☑ Is It True That a Cat Always Lands on Its Feet? Cats possess a genuine righting reflex: specialized inner-ear organs detect orientation during a fall, and a flexible spine twists to bring the feet beneath the body. At sufficient height, this works reliably. A 1987 study of 132 cats brought to a New York veterinary clinic after falls found that injury rates declined in animals falling from higher floors: once terminal velocity is reached at approximately five to six stories, cats relax and spread their limbs, distributing impact more effectively than in shorter, faster falls. The reflex is real and remarkable — but "always" is the myth. Cats sustain serious injuries from falls, particularly at intermediate heights. (Source: Journal of the American Veterinary Medical Association, 1987)

☑ Can Animals Really Predict Earthquakes, and Has Any Researcher Measured It? A 2020 study by the Max Planck Institute of Animal Behavior attached GPS loggers to cows, sheep, and dogs in Italy's earthquake-prone Apennine region. It detected coordinated anomalous movement in all three species beginning six to twenty hours before seismic events, with behavioral intensity correlating to proximity to the epicenter. Similar patterns had been anecdotally reported since ancient Greece. The proposed mechanism — ionized particles released by stressed rock stimulating animal sensory systems — is plausible but lacks direct experimental proof. The behavior exists; the biological pathway producing it remains an open question. (Source: Ethology, 2020)

☑ Does the Scientific Community Now Accept That Fish Feel Pain? For decades, the dominant view held that fish lacked the neocortex required for conscious pain experience. A 2003 study by Lynne Sneddon at the University of Liverpool changed the conversation: rainbow trout injected with acetic acid displayed rocking, fin-rubbing, and suppressed feeding responses reversed by morphine — indicating genuine nociception beyond reflex. By 2021, a scientific consensus had formed recognizing that fish possess functional nociceptors and opioid systems capable of pain-consistent responses through non-neocortical pathways. The question shifted from whether fish feel pain to how that experience compares to mammalian pain. (Source: Proceedings of the Royal Society B, 2003)

☑ **Why Did Physicists Doubt That the Mantis Shrimp Could Weaponize a Physics Phenomenon?** When marine biologists reported that the mantis shrimp's club strike generates cavitation bubbles producing light, heat, and a secondary pressure wave beyond the physical blow, physicists questioned whether any biological structure could create the required hydrodynamic conditions. High-speed analysis at over one million frames per second confirmed it: the club drops local water pressure below its vapor point. These nucleating bubbles collapse at temperatures briefly exceeding 8,000 degrees F (4,400 degrees C). The animal consistently replicates a physics phenomenon previously associated only with industrial propeller damage — at the end of a limb no wider than a pencil. (Source: Journal of Experimental Biology, 2005)

☑ **Does a Cat Purr Solely to Signal Contentment?** The contentment explanation is real but incomplete. Cats purr across a wide range of states, including stress, injury, and labor, indicating a function beyond social signaling. The frequency range of cat purring — 25 to 50 Hz — falls within the range biophysical research associates with stimulating bone density maintenance and accelerating healing of fractures, tendons, and muscle tissue. Veterinary researchers have noted that cats recover from orthopedic injuries at rates disproportionate to their often sedentary recovery conditions, suggesting purring functions as a low-cost, internally generated bone maintenance mechanism during extended inactivity. (Source: Journal of the Acoustical Society of America, 2001)

☑ **Is There Scientific Evidence That Animals Dream?** In 2001, MIT neuroscientists demonstrated that hippocampal neurons in sleeping rats replayed the precise spatial sequences those rats had run hours earlier — in the correct order and at the correct speed — well beyond chance. The same neural structures active during waking navigation fired identically during sleep. Dogs exhibit eye movements, limb twitching, and respiratory irregularities during REM-equivalent sleep consistent with vivid dreaming. Sleeping zebra finches show motor neuron activation matching the exact sequence of songs produced that day. The behavioral and neural evidence for dreaming now spans mammals, birds, and possibly other vertebrate classes. (Source: Neuron, 2001)

☑ What Animal Behavior Discovery Since 2010 has most dramatically overturned a Long-Standing Classification? Crocodilians were formally categorized as behavioral automatons for over two centuries. A 2013 paper documented American alligators and mugger crocodiles in India balancing sticks on their heads during nesting season and positioning themselves beneath active bird rookeries. Because nesting birds collect sticks, the crocodilians were exploiting knowledge of what birds need, when they need it, and where to be — a form of seasonal, tool-assisted luring that had gone undetected in a genus studied formally since the 1700s. (Source: Ethology, Ecology and Evolution, 2013)

☑ How Did Underwater Camera Evidence Overturn a Century of Assumptions About Whale Shark Feeding? Whale sharks were classified as obligate filter feeders — passive animals that swim open-mouthed through plankton. Footage compiled from Western Australia between 2011 and 2015 proved otherwise: whale sharks actively ram-feed into dense baitfish schools at speeds impossible through passive filtration, use suction feeding while hovering vertically, and position themselves near fishing vessels to exploit discarded bycatch. A species watched by divers for decades was an active, opportunistic, adaptive feeder whose behavior had been mischaracterized by observing only one of its feeding modes. (Source: PLOS ONE, 2015)

☑ Which Unexpected Animals Have Joined the Tool-Use Club Since 2000? Before 2000, confirmed tool use was largely confined to great apes and a handful of corvids—the two decades since have expanded that list considerably. In 2009, veined octopuses in Indonesia were filmed carrying coconut shell halves across open seafloor and later assembling them as portable shelters — the first confirmed tool use by any invertebrate. Between 2011 and 2016, tusk fish on Australia's Great Barrier Reef were documented using coral rubble as anvils to crack clam shells, and wrasse performed the same behavior independently in a separate ocean basin. Transporting an object to use it later was no longer exclusively vertebrate. (Source: Current Biology, 2009)

☑ **When Were Crows Proven to Plan a Multi-Step Tool Sequence Without Prior Training on It?** In 2019, University of Cambridge researchers gave New Caledonian crows a problem requiring three tools in a fixed sequence: a short stick, a medium stick, and a longer one, and only the longest reached the food. The birds solved it without training on the specific sequence — only its components. Planning a tool chain in which each step produces no immediate reward requires holding the final goal in working memory across multiple actions. Prior to this study, only humans and some great apes had demonstrated this capacity under controlled conditions. (Source: Current Biology, 2019)

☑ **Why Is the Vampire Squid Neither a Vampire Nor a Squid?** Vampyroteuthis infernalis — Latin for "vampire squid from hell" — was named in 1903 for its dark coloration, red eyes, and cloak-like webbing. It is neither a true squid nor an octopus but the sole living member of its own order, Vampyromorphida, which diverged from both lineages roughly 200 million years ago. Its name implies a predator; the biological reality is a passive detritivore. It descends into oxygen-minimum zones where predators cannot follow and uses retractile filaments to collect marine snow — drifting organic debris from surface waters. It does not hunt, does not bite, and eats only material already dead. (Source: Deep-Sea Research, 2012)

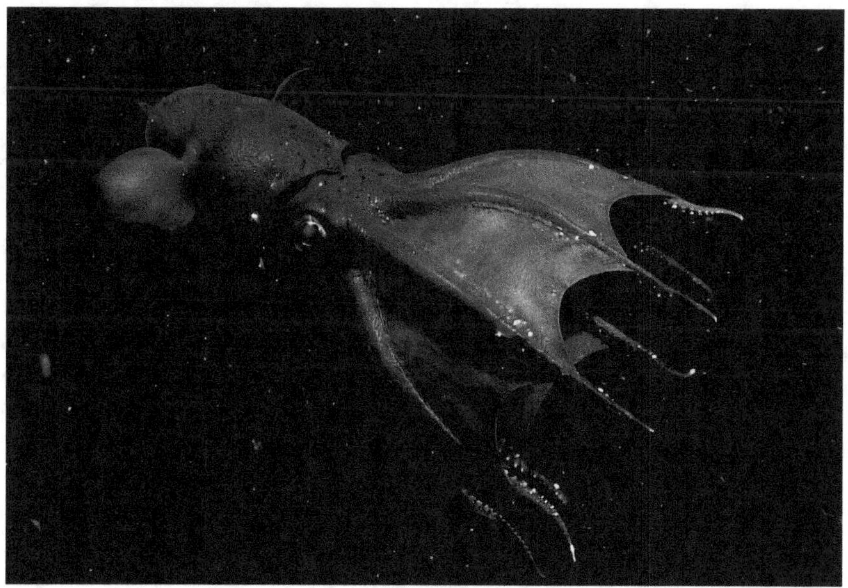

☑ **What Has DNA Testing of Bigfoot and Yeti Physical Evidence Actually Found?** Between 2014 and 2017, two independent research teams — one led by Bryan Sykes at Oxford University, one at the Smithsonian Institution — tested hair samples submitted as Bigfoot, Yeti, and Almas evidence from museums and field investigators across four continents. Every viable sample matched a known species: bears, horses, cows, deer, and raccoons. One Himalayan sample attributed to the Yeti matched a rare Tibetan brown bear subspecies. No evidence from any continent returned DNA consistent with an unidentified primate. Decades of collected material, tested by independent teams, produced zero biological evidence for any undescribed large primate. (Source: Proceedings of the Royal Society B, 2014)

☑ **Must All Sharks Keep Swimming to Breathe?** Some species require continuous forward motion for respiration — a method called obligate ram ventilation in which swimming forces oxygenated water across the gills. Mako and great white sharks fall into this category and suffocate if restrained. Most shark species, however, use buccal pumping: actively working jaw muscles to move water across the gills while stationary. Nurse sharks, wobbegongs, and epaulet sharks rest motionless on the seafloor without respiratory difficulty. The epaulet shark tolerates severe oxygen depletion on tidal reef flats and can walk between pools using its pectoral fins, entirely without swimming. (Source: Journal of Experimental Biology, 1997)

☑ **Why Do Hundreds of Millions of Birds Die Hitting Glass Each Year Despite Superior Eyesight?** The problem is not poor vision. Glass performs two optical functions with no evolutionary precedent in bird history: it transmits interior scenes, creating the illusion of a clear corridor through the building, and simultaneously reflects sky and vegetation, simulating open air. An estimated 600 million birds die annually from building strikes in the United States alone. The solution involves ultraviolet-patterned glass or closely spaced external markers: birds detect UV wavelengths invisible to humans, so UV patterns transparent to people appear as visible barriers to birds, breaking the fatal illusion before contact. (Source: The Condor, 2014)

☑ **What Is the Biggest Unresolved Question in Animal Navigation Research?** Researchers can track exactly where animals migrate with GPS precision. What remains elusive is the cellular mechanism behind magnetic navigation. The cryptochrome hypothesis proposes that quantum-scale electron spin states in retinal proteins allow animals to perceive Earth's magnetic field as a directional visual overlay. This has passed double-blind experimental testing in European robins. But no research team has yet produced neuroimaging of the magnetic sense operating in real time in a freely navigating animal. How a biological molecule translates quantum spin states into directional information remains an open question at the boundary of physics and neuroscience. (Source: Nature, 2021)

☑ **Why Does Neuroscience Lack a Unified Theory of What the Cerebellum Actually Does?** The cerebellum holds approximately 80% of the brain's total neurons and has been defined as the motor-coordination center since the 19th century. That function is confirmed. But imaging studies from 2010 to 2020 consistently activate the cerebellum during language processing, emotional regulation, and abstract prediction tasks having nothing to do with movement. Animals and humans with cerebellar damage show cognitive and emotional deficits that the motor model cannot explain. Despite 150 years of neuroscience, the structure containing the vast majority of the vertebrate brain's neurons has no agreed-upon function beyond the one established at its discovery. (Source: Trends in Cognitive Sciences, 2019)

☑ **Will a Mother Bird Abandon a Chick That a Human Has Touched?** Ornithologists describe this as one of the most harmful wildlife myths because people who believe it leave rescuable chicks unassisted. Most bird species have a limited sense of smell and cannot detect human scent on a chick. Parental behavior is governed by auditory and visual signals from chicks in the nest, not by chemical cues. Returned chicks in field studies are accepted without rejection attributable to handling. No peer-reviewed study of any bird family has documented nest abandonment caused by human contact with a chick. The myth has no evidential basis and causes measurable harm every breeding season. (Source: Cornell Lab of Ornithology, 2014)

☑ Can Cockroaches Survive a Nuclear Explosion? Partly true, substantially overstated. Cockroaches tolerate radiation doses between 6,400 and 10,000 rads — compared to a lethal human dose of roughly 800 rads — because their cells divide slowly, reducing radiation-induced replication errors. Above 10,000 rads, they die within days. The actual radiation champion is Deinococcus radiodurans, a bacterium that survives 1.5 million rads by rapidly reassembling its fragmented genome. A cockroach near a nuclear detonation would not survive the blast overpressure, thermal pulse, or prompt radiation dose. The popular claim describes a real but limited biological tolerance, inflated well beyond the data. (Source: Health Physics Journal, 2004)

☑ Can Sharks Detect a Single Drop of Blood From a Mile Away? The mile-radius claim is not experimentally supported. Sharks detect blood-borne amino acid compounds at concentrations as low as one part per ten billion — roughly a teaspoon dissolved into a large swimming pool. Still, the detection range is constrained by water currents. Sharks navigate a scent concentration gradient along a plume; they follow a trail, not a uniform signal in all directions simultaneously. Controlled measurements support detection over several hundred meters under favorable current conditions. Sensitivity also varies sharply by species: oceanic whitetip sharks demonstrate far higher olfactory acuity than nurse sharks tested under identical conditions. (Source: Florida Museum of Natural History, 2019)

☑ Are Hibernating Animals in an Unbroken Sleep Throughout Winter? The popular image misrepresents a metabolically complex state that is neither continuous nor analogous to sleep. True hibernators such as Arctic ground squirrels drop body temperature to near ambient, reduce heart rate from over 200 beats per minute to fewer than five, and slow respiration to near-zero. But they periodically arouse: ground squirrels wake roughly every one to three weeks, raise body temperature for several hours, then re-enter torpor. These arousals consume the majority of the energy budget, and their function is not fully understood. Bears undergo a lighter torpor from which they can be roused — technically not hibernation. (Source: Journal of Experimental Biology, 2011)

One Last Thing Before You Go

───────────◆───────────

You just finished a book where every single fact was verified — traced back to a real source, not copied from the internet or recycled from another book. That matters more than it used to.

Most "fact books" online are built from unverified claims that have been shared so many times that people assume they're true. This series exists to do the opposite. You know the difference now.

If this book delivered — share your honest thoughts with other readers. A review from someone who actually read it means far more than anything a publisher can say.

Leave Your Review Here

P.S.: Your two free exclusive books are waiting. If you haven't claimed them yet, flip back to the Free Books page and claim.

───────────◆───────────

TRUE VERIFIED FACTS • FUN & INTRIGUING FACTS BOOKS SERIES

Disclaimer

———————— ◆ ————————

The facts in this book are presented as reported in scientific journals, academic publications, and verified sources at the time of publication. While every effort has been made to ensure accuracy, some topics remain under active research and may be subject to future revision as discoveries emerge.

A Note on Images: Some photographs and illustrations in this book have been digitally created or enhanced for educational and illustrative purposes. Due to the nature of the subjects covered, copyright, licensing, or availability restrictions, images may not depict the exact subject, location, species, or object described in a given fact. They are intended to complement and enrich your reading experience, not to serve as precise visual documentation.

Legal Notice: This book is for educational and entertainment purposes only. The author and publisher make no warranties, express or implied, regarding the accuracy, completeness, or currentness of any information or imagery contained herein. Science continuously evolves, and tomorrow's discoveries may refine today's facts.

Limitation of Liability: The author and publisher shall not be liable for any errors, omissions, or damages arising from the use of this information. Readers are encouraged to verify any critical information, measurements, or claims independently.

By reading this book, you acknowledge and accept these terms.

———————— ◆ ————————

TRUE VERIFIED FACTS • FUN & INTRIGUING FACTS BOOKS SERIES

The Facts You Can Actually Trust

In a world flooded with viral myths and unverified "facts," this Series stands apart by delivering **True Verified Facts** – 100% research-backed knowledge from the world's most prestigious sources.

What makes the Fun & Intriguing Facts Books Series different is that every single fact in these books has been meticulously verified through academic publications, peer-reviewed scientific journals, and leading research institutions, including MIT, Stanford, NASA, and other authoritative sources.

Explore the Fun & Intriguing Facts Books Series Collection:

Earth & Space Phenomena | AI & Technology | Money & Economics
Flora & Botanical Wonders | Wildlife & Nature | Weather Science
Lunar Mysteries | Sports Achievements | Time & Traditions
...and many more fascinating topics!

**COLLECT THE FUN & INTRIGUING FACTS BOOKS SERIES.
EXPAND YOUR MIND. TRUST WHAT YOU LEARN**

www.ingramcontent.com/pod-product-compliance
Lightning Source LLC
Chambersburg PA
CBHW061039250726

48653CB00001B/169